TION EDITED BY S. R. MEALING

# The
# it Relations
## and
# Allied Documents

CARLETON LIBRARY  NUMBER 7 / $1.95

# THE
# JESUIT
# RELATIONS
# AND
# ALLIED
# DOCUMENTS

✳✳✳✳

## A SELECTION

✳✳✳✳

# THE JESUIT RELATIONS AND ALLIED DOCUMENTS

\*\*\*\*

## A SELECTION

\*\*\*\*

*Edited and with an Introduction by*

### S. R. MEALING

\*\*\*\*

*The Carleton Library No. 7*

*McClelland and Stewart Limited*

# CONTENTS

✳ ✳ ✳ ✳

INTRODUCTION

# INTRODUCTION

\*\*\*\*

## THE JESUIT RELATIONS
## AND ALLIED
## DOCUMENTS

\*\*\*\*\*\*\*\*\*\*\*\*\*\*\*

On May 22, 1611, Fathers Pierre Biard and Ennémond Massé landed at the little fortified habitation of Port Royal. They were the first Jesuit priests in northern America, and two others soon followed. They were gratified at their reception by the Micmac Indians, one hundred and forty of whom had already been baptized by a secular priest who had come out the year before. The local Micmac chief offered to make war on any of his tribe who resisted baptism. The governor, and the Huguenot traders interested in the new colony, were less co-operative. The Jesuits, taking part in an attempt to found another Catholic colony farther south, were captured by an English freebooter in 1613. One was killed, the others eventually returned to France. This modest and tragically unsuccessful mission was the prelude to the history of the Jesuits in New France.

The Society of Jesus, thus repulsed from the shores of Acadia, was in fact only recently well established in France. The papal bull confirming the order's institution in 1540 had laid no special emphasis on missionary work, but it had required a special vow of obedience to the Pope, which rendered the Jesuits suspect to the dominant Gallican party in the French Church. The Jesuits were soon identified with the Counter-Reformation – the program of reform within the framework of the Church. This identification involved them in bitter theological controversy, especially with the Dominicans. It also led them, in the cause of Catholic humanism, to become innovators in education. Abandoning the mediaeval curriculum, their schools taught what their founder Ignatius Loyola recommended: ". . . along with the knowledge necessary to a good Christian, the humane sciences, from the rudiments of grammar to the highest branches of study. . . ." The college founded at Quebec in 1635 was to continue that tradition. It was as a teaching order that the Society of Jesus established itself in France. In 1618, when the Jesuits finally secured legal recognition at Paris, they maintained forty-eight colleges in France. By that time they had won the favour of the Crown and the patronage of wealthy and influential Catholic laymen. When Henry IV decided that priests should go to Acadia, his Jesuit confessor, Pierre Coton, persuaded him that they should be Jesuits; and the ship that carried them was provided by a royal lady-in-waiting, the Marquise de Guercheville.

When the Récollet friars needed help with their missions in New France, the Jesuits were accordingly well able to provide it. Financed by the viceroy, De Ventadour, a party of Jesuits disembarked at Quebec on June 15, 1625. In ten years the Récollets had gone north to the Montagnais Indians and west to the Hurons; but they could only sketch the ambitious design that the Jesuits had the manpower and funds to fulfil. From Champlain, the founder and governor of Quebec, the Jesuits received not merely co-operation but what amounted to independence. In 1627 Cardinal Richelieu swept away the tangle of conflicting claims and trading privileges that was endangering the colony, vesting its trade and government in a new body, the Company of New France. The company was required to promote settlement by French Catholics only and to support priests. There was an interlude in 1629-32, while an English expedition held Quebec. Then the Jesuits returned, ready for the work defined by a royal patent drafted, but prophetically not issued, to the Récollets: ". . . to establish the said Catholic faith and this to have proclaimed in lands distant, barbarous and strange, where the holy name of God is not invoked. . . ."

The Jesuits' highest hopes were for the Huron mission. The Hurons were a settled people, farmers and traders; "hardly Barbarians, save in name," they seemed to Father Brébeuf, when compared to the semi-nomadic hunters nearer Quebec. In 1639, when a census showed twelve thousand people in the Huron villages, the Jesuits built a permanent headquarters in Huronia. The mission of Ste Marie was a fortified settlement, containing at times up to sixty Frenchmen. It was not dependent on the Hurons; rather, as the danger of Iroquois attack grew, they became dependent on it. In the last two years of its existence (1648-49), Ste Marie gave shelter to nine thousand Hurons. It was a model of the missionary strategy outlined in Father le Jeune's *Relation* for 1634: the plan of establishing permanent mission stations, to which Indian converts could be attracted both by the consolations of religion and the protection of French power, and where they could be taught the elements of European civilization.

The Huron nation melted away before the attacks of its kinsmen, the Iroquois. Among the five nations of the Iroquois league, and especially among the Mohawks, the Jesuits appeared as the emissaries of a rival, not a protecting power. For a time the Onondagas, at least, seemed ready to accept a permanent mission; but the league went to war with the French again in 1658. Itinerant Jesuits risked their lives among the Iroquois until 1708, but the only permanent Iroquois mission was St François-Xavier, built for refugee converts opposite Montreal and later moved to Caughnawaga. In the same way, refugee Hurons had been brought to the safety of Quebec, being settled first on the Isle of Orléans and then at Lorette. St Joseph de Sillery, which was established for the Montagnais in 1637 and was the first of all the refugee missions, attracted other tribes as well. It was moved to St François de Sales, at the falls of the Chaudière River, in 1685. There it became the special refuge of the Abenakis, the centre for itinerant missions southeastward among that tribe, and a strategic point in the vicious border war between New France and New England. The mission station was as apt an instrument for consolidation as for expansion.

From the first, Ste Marie among the Hurons was intended as a base not only for other stations in Huronia but also for missions to neighbouring tribes. Before the first French defeat of the Mohawks (1666-67) these missions had little success, although Jesuits ranged far enough to report on Sault Ste Marie (1641) and Niagara Falls (1648). The far western mission was continuous from the voyages of Fathers Ménard and Allouez. Its base was the station of St Ignace, near Michilimackinac, founded in 1670 by Father Marquette. In his time five hundred Hurons and thirteen hundred Ottawas camped there, refugees from the alternative dangers of the Iroquois and the Sioux. Farther south, Marquette found the populous and tractable Illinois tribes. Before being abandoned for Detroit in 1703, St Ignace spawned a set of still more distant mission stations, ringing southwestern Lake Michigan and pointing the way to the Mississippi and Louisiana.

On the same plan was the expansion northwestward from the mission built at Tadoussac in 1641. It led to mission stations among the Montagnais on Lake St John and at Chicoutimi. Father Albanel reached Hudson Bay by this route in 1671-72. But neither its spiritual nor its secular prospects could compare with those of the upper Great Lakes.

With the discovery of the Mississippi (1673-74), the lead in French expansion passed from the Jesuits to the fur trade and to secular empire-builders. The characteristic problem of the first missionaries had been to win the acceptance of pagan tribes: to acquire the skills of the woodsman; to learn new languages; to endure squalor, privation, fatigue and loneliness; to win a hearing in the face of hostility or ridicule; perhaps to face death. Now the missionary faced new problems, less heroic but more complex: to manage and sustain permanent mission stations; to prevent his converts from barbarizing their new religion; to prevent his countrymen – traders or soldiers – from demoralizing his converts.

This last was a task for statesmen, not for martyrs. Although the extent of the Jesuits' knowledge of the fur trade was recognized, they were not powerful enough to control it. In general, however, the Society of Jesus did not lack for worldly wisdom or influence. Le Jeune's energy and imagination, Vimont's endless close calculations of cost, above all Jérôme Lalemant's wisdom and patience established it as a power in the colony. The estates it accumulated there – nearly 900,000 acres by 1760 – were a compensation for the waning of its influence in France. The Jesuits had their share of bitter and of petty quarrels in New France – with the returned Récollets, with the explorer La Salle, with Governor Frontenac – but their position as the principal missionaries and teachers in the colony was never challenged. It was broken at last by the British conquest and by the papal suppression (1773) of the Jesuit order. For nine years after that final blow the Montagnais and Illinois missions persisted. Later still, the last superior at Quebec was trying, unsuccessfully, to preserve the estates of the order.

The Jesuit missionaries in North America have been abundantly idealized. They were indeed a highly selected body of men; but their archetype is hardly to be found in a martyr like Father Brébeuf, who conducted his mission with such ebullient success and met his cruel death with such fervent courage. There were humbler forms of martyrdom: death by exposure for poor Father de Noüe, relegated to be chaplain to troops because he could not learn Huron; by drowning for Father Ménard; by disease and exhaustion for Father Marquette. Commoner still, and bitterly felt, were the humiliations of Father Davost, that perennially inept traveller; or the grinding discouragement that led Father de Crépieul, after twenty-six years at Tadoussac, to sign himself "an unprofitable servant of the Missions of canada"; or the frustration of Father de Carheil, unable to keep his converts away from brandy. Against the dark background of danger, or of failure, petty torments were more complained of, just as trivial enjoyments were more noted. The journal kept by the Jesuits at Quebec shows livelier displeasure at the trick of a swindler than at an Iroquois massacre, and dwells more on the exchange of New Year's presents than on the destruction of Huronia. The courage of the Jesuits, while great, was matched often enough on the frontier by both red men and white; their religious zeal, while intense, was typical of their century. Eight of them have been declared saints, but the *Relations* show that even the saints were entirely human and therefore entirely interesting.

The original *Relations* were reports from missions, compiled by the Jesuit superior at Quebec and sent to the provincial of the order at Paris. The North American reports were made regularly from 1611 to 1768; those from 1632 to 1673 were published in France and served to publicize the missions. The *Relations* proper, together with a mass of other documents, were edited and translated by the American historian Reuben Gold Thwaites in one of the most comprehensive projects of modern scholarship: *The Jesuit Relations and Allied Documents,* 73 vols. Cleveland: Burrows Brothers, 1896-1901. The present selection is drawn from Thwaites, chiefly by way of the edition prepared by Edna Kenton (New York: Albert and Charles Boni, 1925).

Documents have been chosen to illustrate the coming of the Jesuits, their work as missionaries to the Hurons and to the western tribes, their role in the seventeenth-century expansion of New France, and their life and missionary work in the colony. So far as is possible in a small volume, very short extracts have been avoided, as have documents whose circumstances require special explanation. The text of Thwaites' translation is unchanged except for elisions, which are marked by dots, and some explanatory insertions in square brackets.

S. R. MEALING
*Carleton University*
*June, 1963*

# PART ONE

# THE BEGINNINGS
# OF THE JESUIT MISSION
# TO NEW FRANCE

✳✳✳✳✳✳✳✳✳✳✳✳✳✳

# I

✳✳✳✳✳✳✳✳✳✳✳✳✳

LETTER FROM FATHER CHARLES L'ALEMANT,[1]
SUPERIOR OF THE MISSIONS OF CANADA,
TO THE VERY REVEREND FATHER
MUTIO VITELLESCHI, GENERAL OF
THE SOCIETY OF JESUS, AT ROME
(1626)

✳✳✳✳

VERY REVEREND FATHER IN CHRIST:

The peace of Christ be with you.

Your Paternity need not be surprised to have received no letters
from us during the year since our last; for we are so remote
from the seacoast that we are visited only once a year by French
vessels, and then only by those to whom navigation hither is
allowed, for to others it is interdicted, so that, if by any mis-
chance these merchant ships should be wrecked, or be taken by
pirates, we could look to Divine providence alone for our daily
bread. For from the savages, who have scarcely the necessaries
of life for themselves, nothing is to be hoped; but he who

hitherto provided for the needs of the French, who have dwelt here so many years only with a view to temporal gain, will not abandon his faithful ones who seek only the glory of God and the salvation of souls. During the past year we have devoted ourselves almost entirely to learning the dialect of the savages, excepting a month or two spent in cultivating the soil, in order to obtain such slight means of subsistence as we could. Father Jean Brebeuf,[2] a pious and prudent man, and of a robust constitution, passed the sharp winter season among the savages, acquiring a very considerable knowledge of this strange tongue. We, meantime, learning from interpreters who were very unwilling to communicate their knowledge, made as much progress as we could hope, contrary to the expectation of all. But these are only the rudiments of two languages; many more remain. For the languages are multiplied with the number of the tribes; and this land, extending so far in every direction, is inhabited by at least fifty different tribes, truly an immense field for our zeal. The harvest is great, the laborers are few; but they have, by God's grace, a courage undaunted by any obstacles, although the promise of success is not yet very great, so rude and almost brutish are the natives.

Our labors this year have had no further fruit than a knowledge of the country, of the natives, and of the dialects of two tribes, if the savages alone be considered. As regards the French, whose number does not exceed forty three, we have not been negligent. We have heard their general confessions, relating to their whole past life, after first holding an exhortation on the necessity of this confession. Each month we have, moreover, preached two sermons to them.

We are, God be thanked, all well. . . . Hardly one of us uses bed linen when he sleeps. All our time that is not devoted to seeking the salvation of our fellow men and of ourselves is occupied in tilling the soil. Far greater would be our growth in virtue, if another of Our Brothers were not more desirable as superior. This is easy for Your Paternity to remedy, as I feel myself far better fitted for obedience than for command. I truly hope that Your Paternity, from whom I ask it with all possible submission, will grant me this.

Some workmen have been sent to us this year from France, to construct the first dwelling of the Society here, which we considered as quite indispensable on account of our French, who settle here and nowhere else. Others will be built later among other tribes from whom we expect greater results. To those that have fixed settlements we shall in a short time send one of our number, or rather two: Father Jean de Brébeuf and Father Anne de Noue. If their mission is successful, a most promising field will be opened for the Gospel. They must be taken there by the savages, for they cannot use any other boatmen.

With the consent of his superior, Father Philibert Noyrot returns to France to promote as hitherto the interests of our enterprise. He stands in need of the influence of Your Paternity in order to negotiate freely with those who have charge of our affairs. Our own Father at Paris, for some reason, put difficulties in our way, and seems rather unfriendly to our mission; so that, but for the favor of Father Cotton of blessed memory, our affairs would have fallen to the ground.

As Father Noyrot is to return at the beginning of spring, another of our members will be absolutely necessary at Paris, or at Rouen, to fill his place and to look after our interests, sending us yearly what supplies we need, and receiving our letters, if Your Paternity so decide. There remain thus seven of us here: four priests, Father Enemond Massé, as admonitor and confessor, Father Jean de Brébeuf, Father Anne de Noüe, and myself; and three lay brothers, Gilbert Burel, Jean Goffestre, and François Charreton, all of us ready to undertake any labors whatsoever for the glory of God. We all commend ourselves to the Most Holy Sacrifices of Your Paternity.

Your Paternity's most humble son,

CHARLES LALEMANT.

*New France,*
*August 1st. [1626]*

# II

✳✳✳✳✳✳✳✳✳✳✳✳✳✳

BRIEF RELATION OF THE JOURNEY TO NEW
FRANCE, MADE IN THE MONTH OF APRIL
LAST BY FATHER PAUL LE JEUNE,[3]
OF THE SOCIETY OF JESUS

*Sent to Reverend Father Barthelamy Jacquinot,
Provincial of the same Society,
in the Province of France*

(1632)

✳✳✳✳

MY REVEREND FATHER:

Having been notified by you on the last day of March that I should embark as early as possible at Havre de Grace, to sail directly for New France, I left Dieppe the next day. . . .

We had fine weather at first, and made about six hundred leagues in ten days, but we could hardly cover two hundred on the following thirty three days. I had sometimes seen the angry sea from the windows of our little house at Dieppe; but watching the fury of the Ocean from the shore is quite different from tossing upon its waves. It is one thing to reflect upon death in one's cell, before the image on the Crucifix, but it is quite another to think of it in the midst of a tempest and in the presence of death itself. We found winter in summer; that is to say, in the month of May and a part of June, the winds and the fogs chilled us; Father de Noüe's feet and hands were frozen; and besides this, I had pains in my head or heart, which scarcely left me at all during the first month; and a keen thirst, because we ate nothing but salted food, and there was no fresh water upon our vessel. The size of our cabins was such that we could not stand upright, kneel, or sit down; and, what is worse, during the rain, the water fell at times upon my face. Still it seems to me that I got along better than Father de Nouë, who for a long time, was hardly able to eat. . . .

On Pentecost day, just as I was ready to preach, as I usually did on Sundays and great Fete days, one of our sailors began to cry out, "Codfish! codfish!" He had thrown in his line and had brought out a large one. We had already been on the banks several days, but had caught very little. On that day we drew in as many as we liked. These fresh supplies were very welcome to us after such continuous storms.

On the following Tuesday, the first day of June, we saw land. It was still covered with snow, for the winter, always severe in this country, was extremely so this year. Some days before, we had encountered two icebergs of enormous size, floating upon the sea. They were longer than our ship and higher than our masts, and as the Sunlight fell upon them you would have said they were Churches, or rather, mountains of crystal. I would hardly have believed it if I had not seen it.

On Thursday, June 3rd, we passed into the country through one of the most beautiful rivers in the world. The great Island of newfoundland intercepts it at its mouth, leaving two openings whereby it can empty into the sea. Upon entering, you discover a gulf 150 leagues [450 miles] wide; going further up, where this grand river begins to narrow, it is even there 37 leagues wide. Where we are, in Quebec, distant over 200 leagues from its mouth, it is still half a league wide. . . .

The next day we again set sail, and on the 18th of June we cast anchor at Tadoussac. . . .

It was here that I saw Savages for the first time. As soon as they saw our vessel they lighted fires, and two of them came on board in a little canoe very neatly made of bark. The next day a Sagamore, with ten or twelve Savages, came to see us. When I saw them enter our Captain's room, where I happened to be, it seemed to me that I was looking at those maskers who run about in France in Carnival time. There were some whose noses were painted blue, the eyes, eyebrows, and cheeks painted black, and the rest of the face red; and these colors are bright and shining like those of our masks; others had black, red and blue stripes drawn from the ears to the mouth. Still others were entirely black; except the upper part of the brow and around the ears, and the end of the chin; so that it might have been truly said of them that they were masquerading. There were some who had only one black stripe, like a wide ribbon, drawn from one ear to the other, across the eyes, and three little stripes on the cheeks. Their natural color is like that of those French beggars who are half-roasted in the Sun, and I have no doubt that the Savages would be very white if they were well covered.

To describe how they were dressed would be difficult indeed. All the men, when it is a little warm, go naked, with the exception of a piece of skin which falls from just below the navel to the thighs. When it is cold, or probably in imitation of Europeans, they cover themselves with furs, of the Beaver, Bear, Fox and other animals of the same kind, but so awkwardly, that it does not prevent the greater part of their bodies from being seen. I have seen some of them dressed in Bear skin, just as St. John the Baptist is painted. This fur, with the hair outside, was worn under one arm, and over the other, hanging down to the knees. They were girdled around the body with a cord made of a dried intestine. Some are entirely dressed. They are like the Grecian Philosopher who would wear nothing that he had not made. It would not take many years to learn all their crafts.

All go bareheaded, men and women; their hair, which is uniformly black, is long, greasy, and shiny, and is tied behind, except when they wear mourning. The women are decently covered; they wear skins fastened together on their shoulders with cords; these hang from the neck to the knees. They girdle themselves also with a cord, the rest of the body, the head, the arms and the legs being uncovered. Now that they trade with the French for capes, blankets, cloths, and shirts, there are many who use them, but their shirts are as white and as greasy as dishcloths, for they never wash them. Furthermore, they have good figures, their bodies are well made, their limbs very well proportioned, and they are not so clumsy as I supposed them to be. They are fairly intelligent. They do not all talk at once, but one after another, listening patiently. A Sagamore or Captain, dining in our room one day, wished to say something; and, not finding an opportunity, because they were all talking at the same time, at last prayed the company to give him a little time to talk in his turn, and all alone, as he did.

Now, as in the wide stretches of territory in this country there are a great many wholly barbarous tribes, so they very often make war upon each other. When we arrived at Tadoussac the Savages were coming back from a war against the Hiroquois, and had taken nine of them; those of Quebec took six, and those of Tadoussac three. . . . I went to see them, and found three wooden stakes erected; but news came from Quebec that a treaty of peace was being negotiated with the Hiroquois, and it would perhaps be necessary to surrender the prisoners, and thus their death was delayed. There is no cruelty comparable to that which they practice on their enemies. . . . In short, they make them suffer all that cruelty and the Devil can suggest. At last, as a final horror, they eat and devour them almost raw. If we were captured by the Hiroquois, perhaps we would be obliged to suffer this ordeal, inasmuch as we live with the Montagnards, their enemies. So enraged are they against every one who does them an injury, that they eat the lice and other vermin that they find upon themselves, – not because they like them, but only, they say, to avenge themselves and to eat those that eat them.

Let no one be astonished at these acts of barbarism. Before the faith was received in Germany, Spain, or England, those nations were not more civilized. Mind is not lacking among the Savages of Canada, but education and instruction. They are already tired of their miseries and stretch out their hands to us for help. . . .

The 3rd of July we left Tadoussac and went to cast anchor at the Basque scaffold, a place so called because the Basques go there to catch whales. As it was very calm and we were awaiting the tide, I went ashore. I thought I would be eaten up by the mosquitoes, which are little flies, troublesome in the extreme. The great forests here engender several species of them; there are common flies, gnats, fireflies, mosquitoes, large flies, and a number of others; the large flies sting furiously, and the pain from their sting lasts a long time. The gnats are very small, hardly visible, but very perceptibly felt; the fireflies do no harm; at night they look like sparks of fire, casting a greater light than the glowworms that I have seen in France. As to the mosquitoes, they are disagreeable beyond description. Some people are compelled to go to bed after coming from the woods, they are so badly stung. If the country were cleared and inhabited, these little beasts would not be found here, for already there are but few of them at the fort of Kebec, on account of the cutting down of the neighboring woods.

At length, on the 5th of July, – two months and 18 days since the 18th of April, when we sailed, – we reached the much desired port. We cast anchor in front of the fort which the English held; we saw at the foot of this fort the poor settlement of Kebec all in ashes. The English, who came to this country to plunder and not to build up, not only burned a greater part of the detached buildings which Father Charles Lallemant had had erected, but also all of that poor settlement of which nothing now is to be seen but the ruins of its stone walls. We celebrated the holy Mass in the oldest house in the country, the home of madame Hebert,[4] who had settled near the fort during the lifetime of her husband. She has a fine family, and her daughter is married here to an honest Frenchman. God is blessing them every day; he has given them very beautiful children, their cattle are in fine condition, and their land produces good grain. This is the only French family settled in Canada. They were seeking some way of returning to France; but, having learned that the French were coming back to Quebec, they began to regain courage. When they saw our ships coming in with the white flags upon the masts, they knew not how to express their joy. But when they saw us in their home, to celebrate the holy Mass, which they had not heard for three years, good God, what joy! Tears fell from the eyes of nearly all, so great was their happiness.

The Englishman, having seen the Patents signed by the hand of his King, promised that he would go away within a week, and, in fact, he began preparations for going, although with regret; but his people were all very glad of the return of the French, for they had been given only six pounds of bread, French weight, for an entire week. They told us that the Savages had helped them to live during the greater part of the time. On the following Tuesday, the 13th of July, they restored the fort to the hands of monsieur Emery de Caen and monsieur du Plessis Bochart, his Lieutenant[5]; and on the same day set sail in the two ships that they had anchored here. God knows if our French people were happy, seeing the dislodgment of these

Anglicised Frenchmen, who have done so much injury to these poor countries.

The English dislodged, we again entered our little home. The only furniture we found there was two wooden tables, such as they were; the doors, windows, sashes, all broken and carried away, and everything going to ruin. It is still worse in the house of the Recolet Fathers. We found our cleared lands covered with peas: our fathers had left them to the English covered with wheat, barley, and Indian corn, and meantime this Captain Thomas Ker [Kirk] had sold the full crop of peas, refusing to give them to us for the harvest he had found upon our lands. It is a great deal that such a guest has left our house and the entire country. . . .

I have become teacher in Canada: the other day I had a little Savage on one side of me, and a little Negro or Moor on the other, to whom I taught their letters. After so many years of teaching, behold me at last returned to the A., B., C., with so great content and satisfaction that I would not exchange with my two pupils for the finest audience in France. This little Savage is the one who will soon be left entirely with us. The little Negro was left by the English with this French family which is here. We have taken him to teach and baptize: but he does not yet understand the language well: therefore we shall wait some time yet.

I calculated the other day how much earlier the Sun rises on your horizon than it does on ours, and I found that you have daylight a little over six hours earlier than we do. Our Sailors usually count 17 leagues and a half for a degree of the equinoctial and all other great circles, and otherwise reach the conclusion that there are from here to you 1000 leagues and over, which will consequently make 57 degrees 12 minutes of a great circle upon which we ought to calculate a direct route from here to you. I am writing this about eight in the morning, and it is two in the afternoon where you are. . . .

# III

✲✲✲✲✲✲✲✲✲✲✲✲✲✲✲

## LETTER FROM FATHER PAUL LE JEUNE, TO THE REVEREND FATHER PROVINCIAL OF FRANCE, AT PARIS

*Quebec, 1634*

✲✲✲✲

MY REVEREND FATHER:

The peace of Christ be with you.

. . . I shall spare neither ink nor paper, since Your Reverence endures with so much love my tediousness and simplicity. After having thanked you with all my heart for the help which you have been pleased to send us, as well as for the food and fresh supplies, I will describe to you fully the state of this mission.

Let us begin with what has occurred this year. We have lived in great peace, thank God, among ourselves, with our working people, and with all the french. I have been greatly pleased with all our Fathers. . . .

For the year which we are about to begin at the departure of the ships, this is the way in which we shall be distributed and what we shall do:

Father Brebeuf, Father Daniel,[6] and Father Davost, with three brave young men and two little boys, will be among the Hurons. At last our Lord has opened to them the door. M. Duplessis [-Bouchart] has aided greatly in this; let us say M. de Lauson,[7] who has without doubt recommended this affair to him, of which he has acquitted himself very well, as Your reverence will see by the letter which Father Brebeuf has sent me on his way to the Hurons. I believe that they must now be near the place where they intend to go. This stroke is a stroke from heaven: we shall hope for a great harvest from this country. Father

Brebeuf and Father Daniel exposed themselves to great suffering; for they went away without baggage, or without the money necessary to live. God has provided therefore, as M. Duplessis has taken care that all should go well. So much for the Hurons.

We shall live at Three Rivers, Father Buteux[8] and I. This place is upon the great river, 30 leagues farther up than Kebec, upon the way to the Hurons; it is called Three Rivers, because a certain river which flows through the land empties into the great river by three mouths. Our French people are this year beginning a settlement there, and two of our fathers must be there. I have been doubtful for a long time as to who should go. Father Brebeuf and Father de Noüé thought that I should remain at Kebec, but I perceived that Father Lalemant was apprehensive of this new abode, believing that he would never return if he were sent there, offering himself freely, however, to do what should be desired. It is true that some persons generally die in these beginnings, but death is not always a great evil. . . .

There will remain at Kébec, Father Lallemant, Father Massé, Father de Noüé, and our two Brothers with all our men. The gentleness and virtue of Father Lallemant will hold all in peace, and will cause the work of our people to prosper. . . .

I have said that we lived peacefully on all sides. The murmurs and escapades which occasionally happen should not be placed in the list of great disorders, when one rises as soon as he has fallen, and when the fall is not great. A number of our men have occasionally shown some impatience; but we have reason to bless God, for nothing of importance has happened. Here are the causes for their discontent.

1st. It is the nature of working people to complain and grumble.

2nd. The difference in wages makes them complain; a carpenter, a brickmaker, and others will earn more than the laborers, and yet they do not work so much; I mean that it is not so hard for them as for the others, because they are following their professions, and the others are doing more laborious things. . . . They do not consider that a master-mason may exert himself less than a laborer, although he earns more.

3rd. The greater part do not follow their trades, except for a short time; a tailor, a shoemaker, a gardener, and others, are amazed when required to drag some wood over the snow; besides they complain that they will forget their trades.

4th. It must be confessed that the work is great in these beginnings: the men are the horses and oxen; they carry or drag wood, trees, or stones; they till the soil, they harrow it. The insects in summer, the snows in winter, and a thousand other inconveniences, are very troublesome. The youth who in France worked in the shade find here a great difference. I am astonished that the hardships they have to undergo, in doing things they have never done before, do not cause them to make a greater outcry than they do.

5th. They all lodge in one room; and, as they have not all learned to control their passions, and are of dispositions altogether different, they have occasions for causeless quarrels.

6th. As we are more or less dependent upon them, not being able to send them back when they fail to do right, and as they see that a stick for the purpose of chastising them is of little use in our hands, they are much more arrogant than they would be with laymen, who would urge them with severity and firmness.

Your Reverence will weigh all these reasons, if you please, and will aid us in praising God; for notwithstanding all this, we have not failed to pass the year peacefully, reprimanding some, punishing others, though rarely – very often pretending not to see . . . and, as it is not enough that peace should dwell among us, but that it should be firmly established if it be possible, I deem it best to do what I am about to say.

Only good workmen are needed here; hence it would be well for us to have three capable Brothers, to perform the minor duties of the house – cooking, baking, making shoes, making clothes, looking after the garden, the sacristy, washing, tinkering, caring for the cattle, the milk, butter, etc. All these duties would be divided among these three good Brothers, and thus we would be relieved of giving wages to workmen who are occupied with these duties, and who complain when they are given other things to do. . . .

With these good Brothers, we should have at least ten men capable of building, cultivating, and reaping, – in a word, of doing everything. Whoever could do still more, would be best.

. . . . In regard to the six workmen for whom we ask, the following will be their trades; two strong carpenters, at least one of them understanding how to erect a building, – in a word, let him understand his trade; a joiner, and three workmen who can be employed in clearing the land, in using the pit saw (they need not know this trade, but must have only willingness and strength to do it), in reaping, in helping the carpenters, the mason, the brick maker, in watching the cattle, in doing everything that is required of them; for this, strong men are needed, and those who are willing. If we cannot have two carpenters, let us have one good one, at least, come over; and, instead of the other, such a workman as I have just described. It is very easy to describe a good workman, but quite difficult to find one.

Let us speak of the Fathers whom this mission needs.

Two are needed among the Hurons: if they make peace with the Hiroquois for I am told that it is being negotiated, a number more will be needed, as we must enter all the stationary tribes. If these people receive the faith, they will cry with hunger, and there will be no one to feed them, for lack of persons who know the languages. Moreover, the Brothers who should be among the Hiroquois would exert themselves to preserve the peace between them and the Hurons; nevertheless, on account of the uncertainty of this peace, we ask for only two fathers to go to the Hurons. There must be a superior at Three Rivers, and two Fathers must remain at Kebec, near our french people; so this makes five priests and two Brothers. . . .

My Reverend Father, I beg Your Reverence to discharge me. I sometimes say to the little crosses which come to me, "And this also and as many as you wish, O my God." But to those which Father Lallemant has brought me in Your Reverence's letters, which continue me in my charge, I have said this more than three times, but with a shrinking of the heart which could not drink this cup. In truth, my Reverend Father, I have not the talents, nor the qualities, nor the mildness, necessary to be superior; besides, I say it, and it is true, it is a great disturbance in the study of the language; I say a very great disturbance, – I will even say that this, during the present year, is preventing the salvation, perhaps, of some savages. I learn that the Savages who are at Three Rivers are all sick, and are dying in great numbers. Also Father Brebeuf, who passed through there, writes me that it would be fitting that I should go there; I am busy with the letters, I have nothing or very little ready; the ships will soon be ready to sail away; I shall not have my letters and reports prepared to send Your Reverence in regard to our needs, but I am hurrying as much as possible. . . .

## WHAT MAY BE EXPECTED OF THIS HOUSE FOR THE ASSISTANCE OF THE MISSION, AND THE EXPENSES NECESSARY FOR OUR SUPPORT

There are four staples which make up the greatest expense of this mission; the pork, butter, drinks, and flour, which are sent; in time, the country may furnish these things. As to pork, if from the beginning of this year we had had a building, no more of it, or not much, would have had to be sent next year; we have two fat sows which are each suckling four little pigs, and these we have been obliged to feed all summer in our open court. Father Masse has raised these animals for us. If that point [of land opposite the St. Charles River] . . . were enclosed, they could be put there and during the summer nothing need be given them to eat; I mean that in a short time we shall be provided with pork, an article which would save us 400 livres. As to butter, we have two cows, two little heifers, and a little bull. . . . For lack of a building, they cost us more than they are worth, for our working people are obliged to neglect more necessary things for them; they spoil what we have sown; and they cannot be tended in the woods, for the insects torment them. They have come three years too soon, but they would have died if we had not taken them in; we took them when they were running wild. In time they will provide butter, and the oxen can be used for plowing, and will occasionally furnish meat.

As to drinks, we shall have to make some beer; but we shall wait until we have built, and until a brewery is erected; these three articles are assured with time. As to grains, some people are inclined to think that the land where we are is too cold. Let us proceed systematically, and consider the nature of the soil; these last two years all the vegetables, which came up only too fast, have been eaten by insects, which come either from the neighborhood of the woods, or from the land which has not yet been worked and purified, nor exposed to the air. In midsummer these insects die, and we have very fine vegetables.

As to the fruit trees, I do not know how they will turn out. We have two double rows of them, one of a hundred feet or more, the other larger, planted on either side with wild trees which are well rooted. We have eight or ten rows of apple and pear trees, which are also well rooted; we shall see how they will succeed. I have an idea that cold is very injurious to the fruit, but in a few years we shall know from experience. Formerly, some fine apples have been seen here.

As to the indian corn, it ripened very nicely the past year, but this year it is not so fine.

As to peas, I have seen no good ones here; their growth is too rapid. They succeed very well with this family, who live in a higher and more airy location.

The rye has succeeded very well for two years. We planted some as an experiment, and it is very fine.

Barley succeeds also. There remains the wheat; we sowed some in the autumn at different times; in some places it was lost under the snow, in others it was so preserved that no finer wheat can be seen in France. We do not yet know very well which time it is best to take before winter to put in the seed; the family living here has always sown spring wheat, which ripens nicely in their soil. We sowed a little of it this year, and will see whether it ripens. So these are the qualities of our soil. . . .

Let us come to the spiritual.

First, we shall hope to have in time a great harvest among the Hurons. These people are sedentary and very populous: I hope that Father Buteux will know in one year as much of the montagnais language as I know of it, in order to teach it to the others, and thus I shall go wherever I shall be wanted. These people, where we are, are wandering, and very few in number; it will be difficult to convert them, if we cannot make them stationary.

As to the Seminary, alas! if we could only have a fund for this purpose. . . . We marked out a little space for the beginning of one, waiting until some special houses be erected expressly for this purpose. If we had any built, I would hope that in two years Father Brébeuf would send us some Huron children. They could be instructed here with all freedom, being separated from their parents.

Your Reverence sees, through all that has been said, the benefits to be expected for the glory of God from all of these countries, and how important it is, not only to divert to some other places what is given for the mission at Kebec, but still more to find something which may serve as a retreat for Our Association, as a seminary for the children, and for Our Brothers who will one day learn the language, for there are a great many tribes differing altogether in their language.

Still further . . .

*(The rest of this manuscript is lacking.)*

# IV

✳✳✳✳✳✳✳✳✳✳✳✳✳✳✳

## RELATION OF WHAT OCCURRED IN NEW FRANCE ON THE GREAT RIVER ST. LAWRENCE, IN THE YEAR ONE THOUSAND SIX HUNDRED THIRTY-FOUR

*By Father Paul le Jeune*

## ON THE MEANS OF CONVERTING THE SAVAGES

✳✳✳✳

The great show of power made at first by the Portuguese in the East and West Indies inspired profound admiration in the minds of the Indians, so that these people embraced, without any contradiction, the belief of those whom they admired. Now the following is, it seems to me, the way in which to acquire an ascendency over our Savages.

First, to check the progress of those who overthrow Religion, and to make ourselves feared by the Iroquois, who have killed some of our men, as every one knows, and who recently massacred two hundred Hurons, and took more than one hundred prisoners. This is, in my opinion, the only door through which we can escape the contempt into which the negligence of those who have hitherto held the trade of this country has thrown us, through their avarice.

The second means of commending ourselves to the Savages would be to send a number of capable men to clear and cultivate the land, who, joining themselves with others who know the language, would work for the Savages, on condition that they would settle down, and put their hands to the work, living in

houses that would be built for their use; by this means becoming
located, and seeing this miracle of charity in their behalf, they
could be more easily instructed and won. While conversing this
Winter with my Savages [the Montagnais], I communicated to
them this plan, assuring them that when I knew their language
perfectly, I would help them cultivate their land if I could have
some men, and if they wished to stop roving, – representing to
them the wretchedness of their present way of living, and influ-
encing them very perceptibly, for the time being. The Sorcerer,
having heard me, turned toward his people and said, "See how
boldly this black robe lies in our presence." I asked him why he
thought I was lying. "Because," said he, "we never see in this
world men so good as thou sayest, who would take the trouble
to help us without hope of reward, and to employ so many men
to aid us, without taking anything from us; if thou shouldst do
that," he added, "thou wouldst secure the greater part of the
Savages, and they would all believe thy words."

I may be mistaken but if I can draw any conclusion from the
things I see, it seems to me that not much ought to be hoped for
from the Savages as long as they are wanderers; you will instruct
them today, tomorrow hunger snatches your hearers away,
forcing them to go and seek their food in the rivers and woods.
Last year I stammered out the Catechism to a goodly number
of children; as soon as the ships departed, my birds flew away.
This year, I hoped to see them again, as I speak a little better;
but, as they have settled on the other side of the great river
St. Lawrence, my hopes have been frustrated. To try to follow
them, as many Religious would be needed as there are cabins,
and still we would not attain our object; for they are so occupied
in seeking their livelihood in these woods, that they have not the
time, so to speak, to save themselves.

These reasons, and many others that I might give, were I not
afraid of being tedious, make me think that we shall work a
great deal and advance very little, if we do not make these
Barbarians stationary. As for persuading them to till the soil of
their own accord, without being helped, I very much doubt
whether we shall be able to attain this for a long time, for they
know nothing whatever about it. Besides, where will they store
their harvests? As their cabins are made of bark, the first frost
will spoil all the roots and pumpkins they will have gathered.

If they plant peas and Indian corn, they will have no place in their huts to store them. But who will feed them while they are beginning to clear the land? For they live only from one day to another, having ordinarily no provisions to sustain them during the time that they must be clearing. Finally, when they had killed themselves with hard work, they could not get from the land half their living, until they understood how to make the best use of it.

Now, with the assistance of a few good, industrious men, it would be easy to locate a few families, especially as some of them have already spoken to me about it, thus of themselves becoming accustomed, little by little, to extract something from the earth.

The third means of making ourselves welcome to these people, would be to erect here [at Quebec] a seminary for little boys, and in time one for girls, under the direction of some brave mistress, whom zeal for the glory of God and a desire for the salvation of these people, will bring over here, with a few Companions animated by the same courage. May it please his divine Majesty to inspire some to so noble an enterprise, and to divest them of any fear that the weakness of their sex might induce in them at the thought of crossing so many seas and of living among Barbarians. . . .

## WHAT ONE MUST SUFFER
## IN WINTERING WITH
## THE SAVAGES

. . . . Let us begin by speaking of the house they will have to live in, if they wish to follow them.

In order to have some conception of the beauty of this edifice, its construction must be described. I shall speak from knowledge, for I have often helped to build it. Now, when we arrived at the place where we were to camp, the women, armed with axes, went here and there in the great forests, cutting the framework of the hostelry where we were to lodge; meantime the men, having drawn the plan thereof, cleared away the snow with their snowshoes.

Imagine now a great ring or square in the snow, two, three,

or four feet deep, according to the weather or the place where they encamp. This depth of snow makes a white wall for us, which surrounds us on all sides, except the end where it is broken through to form the door. The framework having been brought, which consists of twenty or thirty poles, according to the size of the cabin, it is planted, not upon the ground, but upon the snow; then they throw upon these poles, which converge a little at the top, two or three rolls of bark sewed together, beginning at the bottom, and behold, the house is made. The ground inside, as well as the wall of snow which extends all around the cabin, is covered with little branches of fir; and, as a finishing touch, a wretched skin is fastened to two poles to serve as a door, the door posts being the snow itself. Now let us examine in detail all the comforts of this elegant Mansion.

You cannot stand upright in this house, as much on account of its low roof as the suffocating smoke; and consequently you must always lie down, or sit flat upon the ground, the usual posture of the Savages. When you go out, the cold, the snow, and the danger of getting lost in these great woods drive you in again more quickly than the wind, and keep you a prisoner in a dungeon which has neither lock nor key.

This prison, in addition to the uncomfortable position that one must occupy upon a bed of earth, has four other great discomforts, – cold, heat, smoke, and dogs. As to the cold, you have the snow at your head with only a pine branch between, often nothing but your hat, and the winds are free to enter at a thousand places. For do not imagine that these pieces of bark are joined as paper is glued and fitted to a window frame; even if there were only the opening at the top, which serves at once as window and chimney, the coldest winter in France could come in there every day without any trouble. When I lay down at night I could study through this opening both the Stars and the Moon as easily as if I had been in the open fields.

Nevertheless the cold did not annoy me as much as the heat from the fire. A little place like their cabins is easily heated by a good fire, which sometimes roasted and broiled me on all sides, for the cabin was so narrow that I could not protect myself against the heat. You cannot move to right or left, for the Savages, your neighbors, are at your elbows; you cannot withdraw to the rear, for you encounter the wall of snow, or the bark of the cabin which shuts you in. I did not know what position to take. Had I stretched myself out, the place was so narrow that my legs would have been half way in the fire; to roll myself up in a ball, and crouch down that way, was a position I could not retain as long as they could; my clothes were all scorched and burned. You will ask me perhaps if the snow at our backs did not melt under so much heat. I answer, "no"; that if sometimes the heat softened it in the least, the cold immediately turned it into ice. I will say, however, that both the cold and the heat are endurable, and that some remedy may be found for these two evils.

But as to the smoke, I confess to you that it is martyrdom. It almost killed me, and made me weep continually, though I had neither grief nor sadness in my heart. It sometimes grounded all of us who were in the cabin; that is, it caused us to place our mouths against the earth in order to breathe; as it were to eat the earth, so as not to eat the smoke. I have sometimes remained several hours in that position, especially during the most severe cold and when it snowed; for it was then the smoke assailed us with the greatest fury. . . .

As to the food, they divide with a sick man just as with the others; if they have fresh meat they give him his share, if he wants it, but if he does not eat it then, no one will take the trouble to keep a little piece for him to eat when he wants it; they will give him some of what they happen to have at the time in the cabin, namely, smoked meat, and nothing better, for they keep the best for their feasts. So a poor invalid is often obliged to eat among them what would horrify him even in good health if he were with our Frenchmen. A soul very thirsty for the Son of God, I mean for suffering, would find enough here to satisfy it.

It remains for me yet to speak of their conversation, in order to make it clearly understood what there is to suffer among these people. I had gone in company with my host and the Renegade, on condition that we should not pass the winter with the Sorcerer, whom I knew as a very wicked man. They had granted my conditions, but they were faithless, and kept not one of them, involving me in trouble with this pretended Magician, as I shall relate hereafter. Now this wretched man and the smoke were the two greatest trials that I endured among these

Barbarians. The cold, heat, annoyance of the dogs, sleeping in the open air and upon the bare ground; the position I had to assume in their cabins, rolling myself up in a ball or crouching down or sitting without a seat or a cushion; hunger, thirst, the poverty and filth of their smoked meats, sickness, – all these things were merely play to me in comparison to the smoke and the malice of the Sorcerer, with whom I have always been on a very bad footing, for the following reasons:

First, because, when he invited me to winter with him I refused; and he resented this greatly, because he saw that I cared more for my host, his younger brother, than I did for him.

Second, because I could not gratify his covetousness. I had nothing that he did not ask me for, often taking my mantle off my shoulders to put it on his own. Now as I could not satisfy all his demands, he looked upon me with an evil eye; indeed, even if I had given him all the little I had, I could not have gained his friendship, because we were at variance on other subjects.

In the third place, seeing that he acted the Prophet, amusing these people by a thousand absurdities, which he invented, in my opinion, every day, I did not lose any opportunity of convincing him of their nonsense and childishness, exposing the senselessness of his superstitions. Now this was like tearing his soul out of his body; for, as he could no longer hunt, he acted the Prophet and Magician more than ever before, in order to preserve his credit, and to get the dainty pieces. So that in shaking his authority, which was diminishing daily, I was touching the apple of his eye and wresting from him the delights of his Paradise, which are the pleasures of his jaws.

In the fourth place, wishing to have sport at my expense, he sometimes made me write vulgar things in his language, assuring me there was nothing bad in them, then made me pronounce these shameful words, which I did not understand, in the presence of the Savages. Some women having warned me of this trick, I told him I would no longer soil my paper nor my lips with these vile words. He insisted, however, that I should read before all those of the cabin, and some Savages who had come thither, something he had dictated to me. I answered him that, if the Apostate would interpret them to me, I would read them. That Renegade refusing to do this, I refused to read. The Sorcerer commanded me imperiously, that is, with high words, and I at first begged him gently to excuse me; but as he did not wish to be thwarted before the Savages, he persisted in urging me, and had my host, who pretended to be vexed, urge me also. At last, aware that my excuses were of no avail, I spoke to him peremptorily, and, after reproaching him for his lewdness, I addressed him in these words; "Thou hast me in thy power, thou canst murder me, but thou canst not force me to repeat indecent words." "They are not such," he said. "Why then," said I, "will they not interpret them to me?" He emerged from this conflict very much exasperated.

In the fifth place, seeing that my host was greatly attached to me, he was afraid that this friendliness might deprive him of some choice morsel. I tried to relieve him of this apprehension by stating publicly that I did not live to eat, but that I ate to live; and that it mattered little what they gave me, provided it was enough to keep me alive. He retorted sharply that he was not of my opinion, but that he made a profession of being dainty; that he was fond of the good pieces, and was very much obliged when people gave them to him. Now although my host gave him no cause for fear in this direction, yet he attacked me at almost every meal as if he were afraid of losing his precedence. This apprehension increased his hatred.

In the sixth place, when he saw that the savages of the other cabins showed me some respect, knowing besides that I was a great enemy of his impostures, and that, if I gained influence among his flock, I would ruin him completely, he did all he could to destroy me and make me appear ridiculous in the eyes of his people.

In the seventh place, add to all these things the aversion which he and all the Savages of Tadoussac had, up to the present time, against the French, since their intercourse with the English; and judge what treatment I might have received from these Barbarians, who adore this miserable Sorcerer, against whom I was generally in a state of open warfare. I thought a hundred times that I should only emerge from this conflict through the gates of death. He treated me shamefully, it is true; but I am astonished that he did not act worse, seeing that he is an idolater of those superstitions which I was fighting with all my might. . . .

One day, when my host had a feast, the guests made me a

sign that I should make them a speech in their language, as they wanted to laugh; for I pronounce the Savage as a German pronounces French. Wishing to please them, I began to talk, and they burst out laughing, well pleased to make sport of me, while I was very glad to learn to talk. I said to them in conclusion that I was a child, and that children made their fathers laugh with their stammering; but in a few years I would become large, and then, when I knew their language, I would make them see that they themselves were children in many things, ignorant of the great truths of which I would speak to them.

Suddenly I asked them if the Moon was located as high as the Stars, if it was in the same Sky; where the Sun went when it left us; what was the form of the earth. (If I knew their language perfectly I would always propose some natural truth, before speaking to them of the truths of our belief; for I have observed that these curious things make them more attentive.) One of them, after having frankly confessed that they could not answer these questions, said to me, "But how canst thou thyself know these things, since we do not know them?" I immediately drew out a little compass that I had in my pocket, opened it, and placing it in his hand, said to him, "We are now in the darkness of night, the Sun no longer shines for us; tell me now, while you look at what I have given you, in what part of the world it is; show me the place where it must rise tomorrow, where it will set, where it will be at noon; point out the places in the Sky where it will never be." My man answered with his eyes, staring at me without saying a word. I took the compass and explained it to him, adding, "Well, how is it that I can know these things, and you do not know them? I have still other greater truths to tell you when I can talk." "Thou art intelligent," they responded, "thou wilt soon know our language." But they were mistaken. . . .

Your Reverence will now see that the fear some people had that the foreigner would again come to ravage the country is not well founded; since households have been established here, since forts and dwellings are being built in several places, and as Monseigneur the Cardinal [Richelieu] favors this enterprise, honorable in the eyes of God and of man. That mind, – capable of animating four bodies, according to what I have heard, – sees far indeed, I confess; but I am of the opinion that he does not expect from our Savages, from this vine, which he waters with his care, the fruits which it will bear for him on earth, and which he will enjoy one day in heaven. God grant that he may see five or six hundred Hurons, – large, strong, well-made men, – ready to listen to the news of the Gospel which is being carried to them this year. I imagine that he would honor occasionally new France by a look, and that this glance would give him as much satisfaction as those great deeds with which he is filling Europe; but to cause the blood of Jesus Christ to be applied to the souls for whom it was shed, is a glory little known among men, but longed for by the great powers of Heaven and earth.

It is time to sound the retreat. The vessels are ready to depart, and still I have not read over and repunctuated this long Relation. Your Reverence will understand that I have not all the leisure that I could desire.

One word more: Give us, my Reverend Father, if you please, persons capable of learning these languages. We intended to apply ourselves to this work this year; Father Lallemant, Father Buteux, and I; but this new settlement separates us. Who knows whether Father Daniel is still living, whether Father Davost will reach the Hurons? For, as his Savages have begun to rob him, they may truly play a still worse game upon him. All this convinces us that we must retain here as many of our Fathers as we can; because if, for example, Father Brébeuf and I should happen to die, all the little we know of the Huron and the Montagnais languages would be lost; and thus they would always be beginning over again, and retarding the fruits that they wish to gather from this mission.

MY REVEREND FATHER,

Your very humble and very obedient servant in Our Lord Jesus Christ,

PAUL LE JEUNE.

*From the little house of N. Dame des Anges in New France, this 7th of August, 1634.*

PART TWO

****

# THE MISSION TO
# THE HURONS

**************

# I

**************

RELATION OF WHAT OCCURRED
AMONG THE HURONS
IN THE YEAR
1635

*Sent to Kebec to Father le Jeune, by Father Brébeuf,
and incorporated in
the Relation for
1635*

****

. . . I arrived among the Hurons on the fifth of August, after being thirty days on the road in continual work, except one day of rest, which we took in the country of the Bissiriniens [Nipissings]. I landed at the port of the village of Toanché or of *Teandeouiata*, where we had formerly lived; but it was with a little misfortune. My Savages, — forgetting the kindness I had lavished upon them and the help I had afforded them in their sickness, and notwithstanding all the fair words and promises they had given me, — after having landed me with some Church ornaments and some other little outfit, left me there quite alone, and resumed their route toward their villages, some seven leagues distant. My trouble was that the village of Toanché had changed since my departure, and that I did not know precisely in what place it was situated. The shore being no longer frequented, I could not easily ascertain my way; and, if I had known it, I could not from weakness have carried all my little baggage at once; nor could I risk, in that place, doing this in two trips. That is why I entreated my Savages to accompany me as far as the village, or at least to sleep on the shore for the night, to watch my clothes while I went to make inquiries. But their ears were deaf to my remonstrances. The only consolation they gave me was to tell me that some one would find me there. Having considered that this shore was deserted, and that I might remain there a long time before any one in the village would come to find me, I hid my packages in the woods; and, taking what was most precious, I set out to find the village, which fortunately I came upon at about three-quarters of a league – having seen with tenderness and emotion, as I passed along, the place where we had lived, and had celebrated the Holy sacrifice of the Mass during three years, now turned into a fine field; and also the sight of the old village, where, except one cabin, nothing remained but the ruins of the others. . . .

I was occupied some two weeks in visiting the villages, and bringing together, at much expense and trouble, all our party, who landed here and there, and who, not knowing the language, could only have found us out after much toil. It is true that one of our men was able to come without any other address than these two words, *Echom, Ihonatiria*, which are my name and that of our village. Among all the French I do not find anyone who has had more trouble than Father Davost and Baron; the Father from the wicked treatment of his Savages, Baron from the length of the journey. He occupied forty days on the road; often he was alone with a Savage, paddling in a canoe very large and very heavily laden. He had to carry all his packages himself; he had narrow escapes three or four times in the torrents; and, to crown his difficulty, much of his property was stolen. Truly, to come here, much strength and patience are needed; and he who thinks of coming here for any other than God, will have made a sad mistake. . . .

Although it is a desirable thing to gather more fruit, and to have more listeners in our assemblies, which would make us choose the larger villages, rather than the small, nevertheless, for a beginning, we have thought it more suitable to keep in the shadow, as it were, near a little village where the inhabitants are already disposed to associate with the French, than to put ourselves suddenly in a great one, where the people are not accustomed to our mode of doing things. To do otherwise would have been to expose new men, ignorant of the language, to a numerous youth, who by their annoyances and mockery, would have brought about some disturbance. . . .

I cannot better express the fashion of the Huron dwellings than to compare them to bowers or garden arbors, – some of which, in place of branches and vegetation, are covered with cedar bark, some others with large pieces of ash, elm, fir, or spruce bark; and, although the cedar bark is best, according to common opinion and usage, there is, nevertheless, this inconvenience, that they are almost as susceptible to fire as matches. Hence arise many of the conflagrations of entire villages. There are cabins or arbors of various sizes, some two brasses [about eleven feet] in length, others of twenty, of thirty, of forty; the usual width is about four brasses, their height is about the same. There are no different stories; there is no cellar, no chamber, no garret. It has neither window nor chimney, only a miserable hole in the top of the cabin, left to permit the smoke to escape. This is the way they built our cabin for us.

The people of Oënrio and of our village were employed at this by means of presents given them. It has cost us much exertion to secure its completion, we were almost into October before we were under cover. As to the interior, we have suited ourselves; so that, even if it does not amount to much, the Savages never weary of coming to see it, and seeing it, to admire it. We have divided it into three parts. The first compartment, nearest the door, serves as an ante-chamber, as a storm door, and as a storeroom for our provisions, in the fashion of the Savages. The second is that in which we live, and is our kitchen, our carpenter shop, our mill, or place for grinding wheat, our Refectory, our parlor and our bedroom. On both sides, in the fashion of the Hurons, are two benches which they call *Endicha*, on which are boxes to hold our clothes and other little conveniences; but below, in the place where the Hurons keep their wood, we have contrived some little bunks to sleep in, and to store away some of our clothing from the thieving hands of the

Hurons. They sleep beside the fire, but still they and we have only the earth for bedstead; for mattress and pillows, some bark or boughs covered with a rush mat; for sheets and coverings, our clothes and some skins do duty.

The third part of our cabin is also divided into two parts by means of a bit of carpentry which gives it a fairly good appearance, and which is admired here for its novelty. In the one is our little Chapel, in which we celebrate every day holy Mass, and we retire there daily to pray to God. It is true that the almost continual noise they make usually hinders us, and compels us to go outside to say our prayers. In the other part we put our utensils. The whole cabin is only six brasses long, and about three and a half wide. That is how we are lodged, doubtless not so well that we may not have in this abode a good share of rain, snow and cold. However, they never cease coming to visit us from admiration, especially since we have put on two doors, made by a carpenter, and since our mill and our clock have been set to work. It would be impossible to describe the astonishment of these good people, and how much they admire the intelligence of the French. No one has come who has not wished to turn the mill; nevertheless we have not used it much, inasmuch as we have learned that our Sagamités[9] are better pounded in a wooden mortar, in the fashion of the Savages, than ground within the mill. I believe it is because the mill makes the flour too fine. As to the clock, a thousand things are said of it. They all think it is some living thing, for they cannot imagine how it sounds of itself; and when it is going to strike, they look to see if we are all there, and if some one has not hidden, in order to shake it.

They think it hears, especially when, for a joke, one of our Frenchmen calls out at the last stroke of the hammer, "That's enough," and then it immediately becomes silent. They call it the Captain of the day. When it strikes they say it is speaking; and they ask when they come to see us how many times the Captain has already spoken. They ask us about its food; they remain for a whole hour, and sometimes several, in order to be able to hear it speak. They used to ask at first what it said. We told them two things that they have remembered very well; one, that when it sounded four o'clock of the afternoon, during winter, it was saying, "Go out, go away that we may close the door," for immediately they arose, and went out. The other, that at midday it said, *yo eiouahaoua*, that is, "Come, put on the kettle;" and this speech is better remembered than the other, for some of these spongers never fail to come at that hour, to get a share of our Sagamité. They eat at all hours, when they have the wherewithal, but usually they have only two meals a day, in the morning and in the evening; consequently they are very glad during the day to take a share with us.

Speaking of their expressions of admiration, I might here set down several on the subject of the loadstone, into which they looked to see if there was some paste; and of a glass with eleven facets, which represented a single object many times, of a little phial in which a flea appears as large as a beetle; of the prism, of the joiner's tools; but above all, of the writing; for they could not conceive how, what one of us, being in the village, had said to them, and put down at the same time in writing, another, who meantime was in a house far away, could say readily on seeing the writing. I believe they have made a hundred trials of it. All this serves to gain their affections, and to render them more docile when we introduce the admirable and incomprehensible mysteries of our Faith; for the belief they have in our intelligence and capacity causes them to accept without reply what we say to them.

It remains now to say something of the country, of the manners and customs of the Hurons, of the inclination they have to the Faith, and of our insignificant labors.

As to the first, the little paper and leisure we have compels me to say in a few words what might justly fill a volume. The Huron country is not large, its greatest extent can be traversed in three or four days. Its situation is fine, the greater part of it consisting of plains. It is surrounded and intersected by a number of very beautiful lakes or rather seas, whence it comes that the one to the North and to the Northwest is called "fresh-water sea." We pass through it in coming from the Bissiriniens. There are twenty Towns, which indicate about 30,000 souls speaking the same tongue, which is not difficult to one who has a master. It has distinctions of genders, number, tense, person, moods; and, in short, it is very complete and very regular, contrary to the opinion of many. . . .

It is so evident that there is a Divinity who has made Heaven and earth that our Hurons cannot entirely ignore it. But they misapprehend him grossly. For they have neither Temples, nor Priests, nor Feasts, nor any ceremonies.

They say that a certain woman called *Eataensic* is the one who made earth and man. They give her an assistant, one named *Jouskeha,* whom they declare to be her little son, with whom she governs the world. This *Jouskeha* has care of the living, and of the things that concern life, and consequently they say that he is good. *Eataensic* has care of souls; and, because they believe that she makes men die, they say that she is wicked. And there are among them mysteries so hidden that only the old men, who can speak with authority about them, are believed.

This God and Goddess live like themselves, but without famine; make feasts as they do, are lustful as they are; in short, they imagine them exactly like themselves. And still, though they make them human and corporeal, they seem nevertheless to attribute to them a certain immensity in all places.

They say that this *Eataensic* fell from the Sky, where there are inhabitants as on earth, and when she fell, she was with child. If you ask them who made the sky and its inhabitants, they have no other reply than that they know nothing about it. And when we preach to them of one God, Creator of Heaven and earth, and of all things, and even when we talk to them of Hell and Paradise and of our other mysteries, the headstrong reply that this is good for our Country and not for theirs; that every Country has its own fashions. But having pointed out to them, by means of a little globe that we had brought, that there is only one world, they remain without reply.

I find in their marriage customs two things that greatly please me; the first, that they have only one wife; the second, that they do not marry their relatives in a direct or collateral line, however distant they may be. There is, on the other hand, sufficient to censure, were it only the frequent changes the men make of their wives, and the women of their husbands.

They believe in the immortality of the soul, which they believe to be corporeal. The greatest part of their Religion consists of this point. We have seen several stripped, or almost so, of all their goods, because several of their friends were dead, to whose souls they had made presents. Moreover, dogs, fish, deer, and other animals have, in their opinion, immortal and reasonable souls. In proof of this, the old men relate certain fables, which they represent as true; they make no mention either of punishment or reward, in the place to which souls go after death. And so they do not make any distinction between the good and the bad, the virtuous and the vicious; and they honor equally the interment of both, even as we have seen in the case of a young man who poisoned himself from the grief he felt because his wife had been taken away from him. Their superstitions are infinite, their feast, their medicines, their fishing, their hunting, their wars, – in short almost their whole life turns upon this pivot; dreams, above all have here great credit.

As regards morals, the Hurons are lascivious, although in two leading points less so than many Christians, who will blush some day in their presence. You will see no kissing nor immodest caressing; and in marriage a man will remain two or three years apart from his wife, while she is nursing. They are gluttons, even to disgorging; it is true, that does not happen often, but only in some superstitious feasts, – these, however, they do not attend willingly. Besides they endure hunger much better than we, – so well that after having fasted two or three entire days you will see them still paddling, carrying loads, singing, laughing, bantering, as if they had dined well. They are very lazy, are liars, thieves, pertinacious beggars. Some consider them vindictive; but, in my opinion, this vice is more noticeable elsewhere than here.

We see shining among them some rather noble moral virtues. You note, in the first place, a great love and union, which they are careful to cultivate by means of their marriages, of their presents, of their feasts, and of their frequent visits. On returning from their fishing, their hunting, and their trading, they exchange many gifts; if they have thus obtained something unusually good, even if they have bought it, or if it has been given to them, they make a feast to the whole village with it. Their hospitality towards all sorts of strangers is remarkable; they present to them, in their feasts, the best of what they have prepared, and, as I have already said, I do not know if anything similar, in this regard, is to be found anywhere. They never close the door upon a Stranger, and, once having received him into their houses, they share with him the best they have; they never send him away, and when he goes away of his own accord, he repays them by a simple "thank you."

What shall I say of their strange patience in poverty, famine, and sickness? We have seen this year whole villages prostrated, their food a little insipid sagamité; and yet not a word of complaint, not a movement of impatience. They receive indeed the news of death with more constancy than those Christian Gentlemen and Ladies to whom one would not dare to mention it. Our Savages hear of it not only without despair, but without troubling themselves, without the slightest pallor or change of countenance. We have especially admired the constancy of our new Christians. The next to the last one who died, named Joseph *Oatij,* lay on the bare ground during four or five months, not only before but after his Baptism, – so thin that he was nothing but bones; in a lodge so wretched that the winds blew in on all sides; covered during the cold of winter with a very light skin of some black animals, perhaps black squirrels, and very poorly nourished. He was never heard to make a complaint. . . .

About the month of December, the snow began to lie on the ground, and the savages settled down into the village. For, during the whole Summer and Autumn, they are for the most part either in their rural cabins, taking care of their crops, or on the lake fishing, or trading; which makes it not a little inconvenient to instruct them. Seeing them, therefore, thus gathered together at the beginning of this year, we resolved to preach publicly to all, and to acquaint them with the reason of our coming into their Country, which is not for their furs, but to declare to them the true God and his son, Jesus Christ, the universal Saviour of our souls.

The usual method that we follow is this: We call together the people by the help of the Captain of the village, who assembles them all in our house as in Council, or perhaps by the sound of the bell. I use the surplice and the square cap, to give more majesty to my appearance. At the beginning we chant on our knees the *Pater noster,* translated into Huron verse. Father Daniel, as its author, chants a couplet alone, and then we all together chant it again; and those among the Hurons, principally the little ones, who already know it, take pleasure in chanting it with us. That done, when every one is seated, I rise and make the sign of the Cross for all; then, having recapitulated what I said last time, I explain something new. After that we question the young children and the girls, giving a little bead of glass or porcelain to those who deserve it. The parents are very glad to see their children answer well and carry off some little prize, of which they render themselves worthy by the care they take to come privately to get instruction. On our part, to arouse their emulation, we have each lesson retraced by our two little French boys, who question each other, – which transports the Savages with admiration. Finally the whole is concluded by the talk of the Old Men, who propound their difficulties, and sometimes make me listen in my turn to the statement of their belief.

Two things among others have aided us very much in the little we have been able to do here, by the grace of our Lord; the first is, as I have already said, the good health that God has granted us in the midst of sickness so general and so widespread. The second is the temporal assistance we have rendered to the sick. Having brought for ourselves some few delicacies, we shared them with them, giving to one a few prunes, and to another a few raisins, to others something else. The poor people came from great distances to get their share.

Our French servants having succeeded very well in hunting, during the Autumn, we carried portions of game to all the sick. That chiefly won their hearts, as they were dying, having neither flesh nor fish to season their sagamité. . . .

YOUR REVERENCE'S:

From our little House of St. Joseph, in the village of Ihonatiria in the Huron country, this 27th of May, 1635, the day on which the Holy Spirit descended visibly upon the Apostles.

> Very humble and obedient
> servant in our Lord,
> JEAN DE BREBEUF.

# II

***************

## INSTRUCTIONS FOR THE FATHERS
## OF OUR SOCIETY
## WHO SHALL BE SENT TO THE HURONS

*(From the* Relation *for 1637,
by Father Jean de Brébeuf)*

****

The Fathers and Brethren whom God shall call to the holy Mission of the Hurons ought to exercise careful foresight in regard to all the hardships, annoyances, and perils that must be encountered in making this journey, in order to be prepared betimes for all emergencies that may arise.

You must have sincere affection for the Savages, – looking upon them as ransomed by the blood of the son of God, and as our Brethren with whom we are to pass the rest of our lives.

To conciliate the Savages, you must be careful never to make them wait for you in embarking.

You must provide yourself with a tinder box or with a burning mirror, or with both, to furnish them fire in the daytime to light their pipes, and in the evening when they have to encamp; these little services win their hearts.

You should try to eat their sagamité or salmagundi in the way they prepare it, although it may be dirty, half-cooked, and very tasteless. As to the other numerous things which may be unpleasant, they must be endured for the love of God, without saying anything or appearing to notice them.

It is well at first to take everything they offer, although you may not be able to eat it all; for, when one becomes somewhat accustomed to it, there is not too much.

You must try and eat at daybreak unless you can take your meal with you in the canoe; for the day is very long, if you have to pass it without eating. The Barbarians eat only at Sunrise and Sunset, when they are on their journeys.

You must be prompt in embarking and disembarking; and tuck up your gowns so that they will not get wet, and so that you will not carry either water or sand into the canoe. To be properly dressed, you must have your feet and legs bare; while crossing the rapids, you can wear your shoes, and, in the long portages, even your leggings.

You must so conduct yourself as not to be at all troublesome to even one of these Barbarians.

It is not well to ask many questions, nor should you yield to your desire to learn the language and to make observations on the way; this may be carried too far. You must relieve those in your canoe of this annoyance, especially as you cannot profit much by it during the work. Silence is a good equipment at such a time.

You must bear their imperfections without saying a word, yes, even without seeming to notice them. Even if it be necessary to criticise anything, it must be done modestly, and with words and signs which evince love and not aversion. In short, you must try to be, and to appear, always cheerful.

Each one should be provided with half a gross of awls, two or three dozen little knives called jambettes (pocket-knives), a hundred fish-hooks, with some beads of plain and colored glass, with which to buy fish or other articles when the tribes meet each other, so as to feast the Savages; and it would be well to say to them in the beginning, "Here is something with which to buy fish." Each one will try, at the portages, to carry some little thing, according to his strength; however little one carries, it greatly pleases the savages, if it be only a kettle.

You must not be ceremonious with the Savages, but accept the comforts they offer you, such as a good place in the cabin. The greatest conveniences are attended with very great inconvenience, and these ceremonies offend them.

Be careful not to annoy anyone in the canoe with your hat; it would be better to take your nightcap. There is no impropriety among the Savages.

Do not undertake anything unless you desire to continue it; for example, do not begin to paddle unless you are inclined to continue paddling. Take from the start the place in the canoe that you wish to keep; do not lend them your garments, unless you are willing to surrender them during the whole journey. It is easier to refuse at first than to ask them back, to change, or to desist afterwards.

Finally, understand that the Savages will retain the same opinion of you in their own country that they will have formed on the way; and one who has passed for an irritable and troublesome person will have considerable difficulty afterwards in removing this opinion. You have to do not only with those of your own canoe, but also (if it must be so stated) with all those of the country; you meet some today and others tomorrow, who do not fail to inquire, from those who brought you, what sort of man you are. It is almost incredible, how they observe and remember even the slightest fault. When you meet Savages on the way, as you cannot yet greet them with kind words, at least show them a cheerful face, and thus prove that you endure gayly the fatigues of the voyage. You will thus have put to good use the hardships on the way, and have already advanced considerably in gaining the affection of the Savages.

This is a lesson which is easy enough to learn, but very difficult to put into practice; for, leaving a highly civilized community, you fall into the hands of barbarous people who care but little for your Philosophy of your Theology. All the fine qualities which might make you loved and respected in France are like pearls trampled under the feet of swine, or rather mules, which utterly despise you when they see that you are not as good pack animals as they are. If you could go naked, and carry the load of a horse upon your back, as they do, then you would be wise according to their doctrine, and would be recognized as a great man, otherwise not. Jesus Christ is our true greatness; it is He alone and His cross that should be sought in running after these people, for, if you strive for anything else, you will find naught but bodily and spiritual affliction. But having found Jesus Christ in His cross, you have found the roses in the thorns, sweetness in bitterness, all in nothing.

# III

✳✳✳✳✳✳✳✳✳✳✳✳✳✳✳✳

## RELATION OF WHAT OCCURRED IN THE MISSION OF THE SOCIETY OF JESUS, IN THE LAND OF THE HURONS, IN THE YEAR 1637

*Sent to Kebec to the Reverend Father Paul le Jeune, Superior of the Missions of the Society of Jesus, in New France.*

*By Father François-Joseph le Mercier*[10]

## THE EXCESSIVE CRUELTY OF MEN, AND THE GREAT MERCY OF GOD, UPON THE PERSON OF A PRISONER OF WAR FROM THE IROQUOIS NATION

✳✳✳✳

On the 2nd of September, we learned that an Iroquois prisoner had been brought to the village of Onnentisati, and that they were preparing to put him to death. This Savage was one of eight captured by them at the lake of the Iroquois; the rest had saved themselves by flight. At first we were horrified at the thought of being present at this spectacle, but, having well considered all, we judged it wise to be there, not despairing of being able to win this soul for God. . . . So we entered and placed ourselves near him; the Father Superior took occasion to tell him to be of good cheer; that he would in truth be miserable during the little of life that remained to him, but that, if he would listen to him, and would believe what he had to tell him, he would assure him of an eternal happiness in Heaven after his death.

Seeing that the hour of the feast was drawing near, we withdrew into the cabin where we had taken lodgings, not expecting to find an opportunity to speak further with him until the next day. But we were greatly astonished and much rejoiced when we were told that he was coming to lodge with us. And still more so afterwards, when the Father Superior had all the leisure necessary to instruct him in our mysteries, – in a word, to prepare him for Holy Baptism. A goodly band of Savages who were present, not only did not interrupt him, but even listened to him with close attention. What a great advantage it is to have mastered their language, to be loved by these people, and to have influence for them! I do not think the Christian truths have ever been preached in this country on an occasion so favorable, for there were present some from nearly all the nations who speak the Huron tongue. The Father Superior found him so well-disposed that he did not consider it advisable to postpone any longer his baptism. This being accomplished, we withdrew from his presence to take a little rest. For my part it was almost impossible for me to close my eyes.

The next morning, the prisoner again confirmed his wish to die a Christian, and he even promised the Father that he would remember to say, in his torments, "Jesus taïtenr," "Jesus, have pity on me." About noon he made his Astataion, that is, his farewell feast, according to the custom of those who are about to die. . . .

## THE HELP WE HAVE GIVEN TO
## THE SICK OF OUR VILLAGE

This is the order we maintained. We visited them twice a day, morning and evening, and carried them soup and meat. We ate during our own sickness a few of the raisins and prunes and some little remedies that your Reverence had sent us, – using them only in cases of necessity, so that we still had a good part of them, which we have made last up to the present. Everything was given by count, two or three prunes, or 5 or 6 raisins to one patient; this was restoring life to him. Our medicines produced effects which dazzled the whole country, and yet I leave you to imagine what sort of medicines they were. A little bag of senna served over 50 persons; they asked us for it on every side. . . .

# IV

✳✳✳✳✳✳✳✳✳✳✳✳✳✳✳✳

LETTER OF FATHER FRANÇOIS DU PERON OF
THE SOCIETY OF JESUS, TO FATHER JOSEPH
IMBERT DU PERON, HIS BROTHER,
RELIGIOUS OF THE SAME
SOCIETY

*At the village of la Conception de Nostre Dame,
this 27 of April, 1639.*

✳✳✳✳

MY REVEREND FATHER:

Pax Christi

. . . . I left Three Rivers on the 4th of September, and reached
the Huron country on the day of Saint Michel [September
29]. . . .

Along the way we passed three wandering Algonquin tribes:
for the rest, forests and bare rocks, rapids and precipices: I am
surprised that the savages dare undertake such a journey. As for
the Huron country, it is tolerably level, with many prairies,
many lakes, many villages; of the two where we are, one contains
80 cabins, the other 40. In each cabin there are five fireplaces,
and two families at each. Their cabins are made of large sheets
of bark in the shape of an arbor, long, wide, and high in
proportion; some of them are 70 feet long. Their land produces
nothing but Indian corn, beans, and squashes. These are the
delicacies of the country, which has nothing in common with
our France, as to things to be enjoyed, except the four elements.
One sees here, nevertheless, birds, fish, and forest animals,
almost the same kinds as in France. The land, as they do not
cultivate it, produces for only ten or twelve years at most; and

when the ten years have expired, they are obliged to move their village to another place.

The nature of the Savage is patient, liberal, hospitable; but importunate, visionary, childish, thieving, lying, deceitful, licentious, proud, lazy; they have among them many fools, or rather lunatics and insane people. . . .

They nearly all show more intelligence in their business, speeches, courtesies, intercourse, tricks, and subtleties, than do the shrewdest citizens and merchants in France. They regulate the seasons of the year by the wild beasts, the fish, the birds, and the vegetation; they count the years, days, and months by the moon.

There are ten of Ours here in two Residences, one at la Conception de Notre Dame, the other at Saint Joseph; these are distant from each other five or six leagues. We expect soon to establish a third Residence in the tobacco nation, without detriment to the itinerant missions. We have with us twelve Frenchmen, who are hired by us. We are lodged and fed in the manner of the savages; we have no land of our own, except a little borrowed field, where French grain is raised just to make the host for the holy mass; we leave the rest to divine Providence, which sends us more corn than if we had broad lands; one person will bring us three ears of corn, another six, some one else a squash; one will give us some fish, another some bread baked under the ashes. As their presents, we give them little glass beads, rings, awls, small pocket knives, and colored beads; this is all our money. As for the delicacies of France, we have none of them here; the usual sauce with the food is pure water, juice of corn or of squashes. The fresh food that comes from France does not go farther up than Three Rivers; all they can send is some church ornaments, some wine for the mass (only four or five drops of it is put into the chalice), and some clothes, some prunes, and raisins for the sick of the village; it all runs great risks on the way. We lost this year two of our packages. Our plates, although of wood, cost us more than yours; for they are valued at one beaver robe, which is a hundred francs. . . .

The importunity of the savages, – who are continually about us in our cabin, – does not prevent our observance of our hours, as well regulated as one of our colleges in France. At four o'clock the rising bell rings; then follows the orison, at the end of which the masses begin and continue until eight o'clock. At eight o'clock the door is left open to the savages, until four in the evening; it is permitted to talk with the savages at this time, as much to instruct them as to learn their language. In this time, also, the Fathers visit the cabins of the town. Then follows dinner. We dine around the fire, seated on a log, with our plates on the ground.

On the 13th of November, the Reverend Father Superior [le Mercier] left here with one of our Fathers, to begin the itinerant missions. The devil seemed to try to oppose their plan; the snow fell so abundantly as to cover all the paths.

On the 2nd of March, and other days following the carnival, the devil was unchained here as well as in France. There was only deviltry and masquerading at that time throughout the Huron country; I will content myself with touching incidentally upon the deviltries of these peoples.

1. All their actions are dictated to them directly by the devil, who speaks to them, now in the form of a crow or some similar bird, now in the form of a flame or a ghost, and all this in dreams, to which they show great deference. They consider the dream as the master of their lives, it is the God of the country. It is this which dictates to them their feasts, their hunting, their fishing, their war, their trade with the French, their remedies, their dances, their games, their songs.

2. To cure a sick person, they summon the sorcerer, who without acquainting himself with the disease of the patient, sings, and shakes his tortoise shell; he gazes into the water and sometimes into the fire, to discover the nature of the disease. Having learned it, he says that the soul of the patient desires, for his recovery, to be given a present of such or such a thing, – of a canoe, for example, of a new robe, a porcelain collar, a fire-feast, a dance, etc., and the whole village straightway sets to work to carry out to the letter all the sorcerer may have ordered. As I was writing this, a Savage, greatly excited, came from a neighboring village, and begged us to give him a piece of red stuff, because the sorcerer had said that one of his sons, who was sick, desired for his recovery this bit of stuff. It was not given to him; but one of our fathers immediately repaired to the place, and baptized the little patient.

3. Nearly all the Savages have charms, to which they speak and make feasts, in order to obtain from them what they desire.

4. The devil has his religious; those who serve him must be deprived of all their possessions, they must abstain from women, they must obey perfectly all that the devil suggests to them. The sorcerer of this village came to see us, and told us all these things.

The number of those baptized this year reaches fully 300 souls; in this village of la Conception, there have been baptized in sickness, both children and others, one hundred and twenty-two persons. Besides the sick, fifty persons in health were solemnly baptized. In the village of St. Joseph, one hundred and twenty-six; in the itinerant mission of St. Michel, twenty-six or seven. I speak only of this country of the Hurons; as concerns Kebec and Three Rivers, you have the Relation of those before we do.

I am with all my heart,
My Reverend Father,
your very humble and very affectionate brother in our Lord,

FRANÇOIS DU PERON,
surnamed in Huron
ANONCHIARA, S.J.

# PART THREE

# THE MARTYRDOM OF HURONIA
## AND
# THE MISSION TO THE IROQUOIS

✱✱✱✱✱✱✱✱✱✱✱✱✱✱✱✱

# I

✱✱✱✱✱✱✱✱✱✱✱✱✱✱✱✱

## OF INCURSIONS BY THE IROQUOIS

*(From the* Relation *for 1642-43,
by Father Barthélémy Vimont*[11])

✱✱✱✱

There are two divisions of Iroquois, – the one, neighbours of the Hurons and equal to them in number, or even greater, are called Santweronons [Senecas]. Formerly the Hurons had the upper hand; at present these prevail, both in number and in strength. The others live between the three Rivers and the upper Hiroquois, and are called Agneronons [Mohawks]. The settlement of the Dutch is near them; they go thither to carry on their trades, especially in arquebuses; they have at present three hundred of these, and use them with skill and boldness. These are the ones who make incursions upon our Algonquins and Montagnais, and watch the Hurons at all places along the River, – slaughtering them, burning them, and carrying off their Peltry, which they sell to the Dutch, in order to have powder and Arquebuses, and then to ravage everything and become masters everywhere, which is fairly easy for them unless France gives us help. For, sundry contagious diseases having consumed the greater part of the Montagnais and the Algonquins, who are neighbors to us, they have nothing to fear on that side; and, moreover, the Hurons who come down, – coming for trade and not for war, and having not one Arquebus, – if they are met, have no other defense than flight; and, if they are captured, they allow themselves to be bound and massacred like sheep.

In former years, the Iroquois came in rather large bands at certain times in the Summer, and afterwards left the River free; but this present year, they have changed their plan, and have separated themselves into small bands of twenty, thirty, fifty, or a hundred at the most, along all the passages and places of the River, and when one band goes away, another succeeds it. They are merely small troops well armed, which set out incessantly, one after the other, from the country of the Iroquois, in order to occupy the whole great River, and to lay ambushes along it everywhere; from these they issue unexpectedly, and fall indifferently upon the Montagnais, Algonquins, Hurons, and French.

We have had letters from France that the design of the Dutch is to have the French harassed by the Iroquois, to such an extent that they may constrain them to give up and abandon everything. I cannot believe that those Gentlemen of Holland, being so united to France, have this wretched idea; but the practice of the Iroquois being so consistent with it, they ought to apply to it a remedy in their settlement, as Monsieur the Governor has done here – often preventing our Savages from going to kill the Dutch. . . .

# II

✳✳✳✳✳✳✳✳✳✳✳✳✳✳✳

## HOW FATHER JOGUES WAS TAKEN BY THE IROQUOIS, AND WHAT HE SUFFERED ON HIS FIRST ENTRANCE INTO THEIR COUNTRY

*(From the* Relation *for 1647, by Father Jérôme Lalemant[12])*

✳✳✳✳

Father Isaac Jogues had sprung from a worthy family of the City of Orleans. After having given some evidence of his virtue in our Society, he was sent to New France, in the year 1638. In the same year he went up to the Hurons, where he sojourned until the thirteenth of June in the year 1642, when he was sent to Kebec upon the affairs of that important and arduous Mission.

From that time until his death, there occurred many very remarkable things, – of which one cannot, without guilt, deprive the public. What has been said of his labors in the preceding Relations, come, for the most part, from some Savages, companions in his sufferings. But what I am about to set down has issued from his own pen and his own lips.

The Reverend Father Hiersome [Jérôme] L'alemant, at that time Superior of the Mission among the Hurons, sent for him, and proposed to him the journey to Kebec, – a frightful one, on account of the difficulty of the roads, and very dangerous because of the ambuscades of the Hiroquois, who massacred, every year, a considerable number of the Savages allied to the French. Let us hear him speak upon his subject and upon the result of his journey:

*Authority having made me a simple proposition, and not a*

*command, to go down to Kebec, I offered myself with all my heart. So there we were, on the way and in the dangers all at once. We were obliged to disembark forty times, and forty times to carry our boats and all our baggage amid the currents and waterfalls that one encounters on this journey of about three hundred leagues. At last, thirty-five days after our departure from the Hurons, we arrived, much fatigued, at Three Rivers; thence we went down to Kebec. Our affairs being finished in fifteen days, we solemnly observed the feast of St. Ignace; and the next day, we left Three Rivers, in order to go up again to the country whence we came. The first day was favorable to us; the second caused us to fall into the hands of the Iroquois.*

*We were forty persons, distributed in several canoes; the one which kept the vanguard, having discovered on the banks of the great river some tracks of men, recently imprinted on the sand and clay, gave us warning. A landing was made: some say that these are footprints of the enemy, others are sure that they are those of Algonquins, our allies. In this dispute, Eustache Ahatsistari exclaimed: "Be they friends or enemies, it matters not; they are not in greater number than we; let us advance and fear nothing."*

*We had not yet made a half-league, when the enemy, concealed among the grass and brushwood, rises with a great outcry, discharging at our canoes a volley of balls. The noise so greatly frightened a part of our Hurons that they abandoned their canoes and weapons in order to escape by flight into the depth of the woods. We were four French, – one of whom, being in the rear, escaped with the Hurons, who abandoned him before approaching the enemy. Eight or ten, both Christians and Catechumens, joined us; they oppose a courageous front to the enemy. But, having perceived that another band – of forty Hiroquois, who were in ambush on the other side of the river – was coming to attack them, they lost courage; insomuch that those who were least entangled fled.*

*A Frenchman named René Goupil, whose death is precious before God, was surrounded and captured, along with some of the most courageous Hurons. I was watching this disaster,* says the Father, *from a place very favourable for concealing me from the sight of the enemy, but this thought could never enter my mind. "Could I indeed," I said to myself, "abandon our*

French and leave those good Neophytes and those poor Cate-chumens, without giving them the help which the Church of my God has entrusted to me?" Flight seemed horrible to me. "It must be," I said in my heart, "that my body suffer the fire of earth, in order to deliver these poor souls from the flames of Hell; it must die a transient death, in order to procure for them an eternal life." My conclusion being reached without great opposition from my feelings, I call the one of the Hiroquois who had remained to guard the prisoners. He advances and, having seized me, puts me in the number of those whom the world calls miserable. . . .

It is a belief among these Barbarians that those who go to war are the more fortunate in proportion as they are cruel toward their enemies; I assure you that they made us thoroughly feel the force of that wretched belief. . . .

# III

\*\*\*\*\*\*\*\*\*\*\*\*\*\*\*

LETTER OF FATHER PAUL RAGUENEAU[13] TO
THE VERY REVEREND FATHER VINCENT
CARAFFA, GENERAL OF THE SO-
CIETY OF JESUS, AT ROME

(1649)

\*\*\*\*

OUR VERY REVEREND FATHER IN CHRIST:

*Pax Christi*

I have received, very Reverend Paternity, your letter dated
January 20, 1647. If you wrote us last year, 1648, we have not
yet received that letter. Your Paternity evinces pleasure in the
news of the state of our Huron mission. Indeed (such is your
Paternal love toward us), you even stoop to details and bid us
inform you of everything.

There are here eighteen Fathers, four coadjutors, twenty-
three Données,[14] seven servants (to whom alone wages are
paid), four boys and eight soldiers. Truly, we are so threatened
by the hostile rage of our savage enemies that, unless we wish
our enterprise and ourselves to perish in an hour, it was quite
necessary for us to seek the protection of these men, who devote
themselves to both domestic duties and farm work, and also to
building fortifications, and to military service. For since, until
late years, our abode, which we call the Residence of Ste. Marie,
was surrounded on every side by the numerous villages of our
friends, the Hurons, we feared more for them than for ourselves
from hostile attack: so during that time, however small our
number, we lived in safety, without anxiety. But now, far
different is the aspect of our affairs and of this whole region;
for so crushed are our Hurons by disasters, that, their outposts
being taken and laid waste with fire and sword, most of them

have been forced to change their abodes, and retreat elsewhere; hence it has come to pass that at last we are devoid of the protection of others; and now we, stationed at the front, must defend ourselves with our own strength, our own courage, and our own numbers.

This our dwelling – or shall I say our fort? – of Sainte Marie, the French who are with us defend, while our Fathers sally forth, far and wide, scattered among the villages of the Hurons, and through the Algonquin tribes far distant from us, – each one watching over his own mission, and intent only upon the ministry of the word, leaving all temporal cares to those who remain at home. In truth, domestic matters keep so fortunate a course that, although our number has increased, and we greatly desire new help to be sent us, – both of laymen and, especially, of our own fathers, – still in no wise is it necessary to increase expenses. On the contrary, they are lessening daily, and each year we ask for less temporal aid to be sent us – so much so that we can, for the most part, support ourselves upon that which is here produced. Verily, there is not one of our brethren who does not feel in this respect great relief from those distresses which were in former years very burdensome, and seemed insurmountable. For we have larger supplies from fishing and hunting than formerly; and we have not merely fish and eggs, but also pork, and milk products, and even cattle, from which we hope for great addition to our store. I write of these particulars, because your Paternity so desired.

Christianity has certainly made progress here, in many ways, beyond our expectation. We baptized, the past year, about one thousand seven hundred, – not counting many whom we shall mention below as baptized by Father Antoine Daniel, the number of whom could not be accurately given. Nor are these, albeit barbarians, such Christians as one might be inclined to suppose, ignorant of things divine and not sufficiently qualified for our mysteries. Many indeed understand religion, and that profoundly; and there are some whose virtue, piety, and remarkable holiness even the most holy Religious might without sin envy. One who is an eye-witness of these things cannot sufficiently admire the finger of God, and congratulate himself that so fortunate a field of labor, so rich in divine blessing, had fallen to his lot.

We maintain eleven missions – eight in the Huron language and three Algonquin. The work is divided between an equal number of Fathers who have had experience. Four, sent to us last year, devote their time to learning the language; and these we have assigned as helpers to the chief missionaries. Thus only three Fathers remain at home – one as spiritual Director, another as Procurator and minister, the third to look after the needs of the Christians, who come to us from every quarter. For out of our own poverty we minister to the poverty of the Christians, and heal their diseases both of soul and body, surely to the great advancement of Christianity. Last year, nearly six thousand partook of our hospitality. I say these things that your Paternity may know the abundance of God's goodness toward us. For, while during this year famine has been heavy upon the villages on all sides of us, and now weighs upon them even more heavily, no blight of evil has fallen upon us; nay, we have enough provisions upon which to live comfortably during three years.

But one thing – the fear of war and the rage of foes – seems able to overthrow the happy state of this infant church, and stay the advance of Christianity; for it grows yearly, and it is clear that no help can come to us save from God alone. The latest disaster that befell our Hurons – in July of last year, 1648 – was the severest of all. Many of them had made ready to visit our French people in the direction of Quebec, to trade; other tasks had drawn some away from their villages; while many had undertaken a hostile expedition in another direction; when suddenly the enemy came upon them, stormed two villages, rushed into them, and set them on fire. With their wonted cruelty they dragged into captivity mothers with their children, and showed no mercy to any age.

Of these villages, one was called Saint Joseph; this was one of our principal missions, where a church had been built, where the people had been instructed in Christian rites, and where the faith had taken deep root. In charge of this Church was Father Antoine Daniel, a man of great courage and endurance, whose gentle kindness was conspicuous among his great virtues. He had hardly finished the usual mass after sunrise; and the Christians, who had assembled in considerable numbers, had not yet left the sacred house, when, at the war-cry of the enemy, in haste and alarm they seized their weapons. Some rush into the fight, others flee headlong; everywhere is terror, everywhere lamentation.

Antoine hastened wherever he saw the danger most threatening, and bravely encouraged his people – inspiring not only the Christians with Christian strength, but many unbelievers with faith. He was heard to speak of contempt for death, and of the joys of Paradise, with such ardor of soul that he seemed already to enjoy his bliss. Indeed, many sought baptism; and so great was the number that he could not attend to each one separately; but was forced to dip his handkerchief in the water and baptize by sprinkling the multitude who thronged around him. . . .

That he may delay the enemy, and, like a good shepherd, aid the escape of his flock, he blocks the way of the armed men and breaks their onset; a single man against the foe, but verily filled with divine strength, he, who during all his life had been as the gentlest dove, was brave as a Lion while he met death. Truly, I might apply to him that saying of Jeremias: "He hath forsaken his covert as the Lion, for the land is laid waste because of the wrath of the dove, and because of the fierce anger of the Lord." At last he fell, mortally wounded by a musket shot; and, pierced with arrows, he yielded to God the blessed life which he laid down for his flock, as a good Shepherd, calling upon the name of Jesus. Savagely enraged against his lifeless body, hardly one of the enemy was there who did not add a new wound to his corpse; until at length, the church having been set on fire, his naked body cast into the flames was so completely consumed that not even a bone was left: indeed, he could not have found a more glorious funeral pyre.

In thus delaying the enemy, he was serviceable to his flock, even after his death. Many reached places of safety; others the victors overtook, especially mothers – at every step delayed by the babes at their breasts, or by those whose childish years – as yet unaccustomed to prudent fear – betrayed their hiding places.

Antoine had just finished his fourteenth year at the Huron mission, everywhere a useful man, and assuredly raised up for the salvation of those tribes; but certainly ripe for heaven, and the first man of our society to be taken from us. True, his death was sudden, but did not find him unprepared: for he had always so lived that he was ever ready for death. Yet the Divine

Goodness toward him seems to have been remarkable; for he had finished, only the first day of July, eight days of continuous spiritual Exercises of the Society in this house of Sainte Marie; and on the very next day, without any delay, or even one day's rest, he hastened to his own mission. Verily he burned with a zeal for God more intense than any flame that consumed his body. . . .

To make an end of writing, without exceeding the limit of a letter, I will add – what should have been written first of all to Your Paternity – that such is the condition of this house, and indeed of the whole mission, that I think hardly anything could be added to the piety, obedience, humility, patience, and charity of our brethren, and to their scrupulous observance of the rules. We are all of one heart, one soul, one spirit of the society. Nay, what must seem more wonderful, out of all the men attached to the house, of condition and nature so varied, – servants, boys, données, soldiers, – there is not one who does not seriously attend to his soul's salvation; so that clearly vice is banished hence, here virtue rules, and this is seen to be the home of holiness. This surely is our rejoicing, our peace in war, and our great security; for, whatever may be the dispensation of divine Providence, in life or in death this will be our consolation, that we are the Lord's and ever shall be, as we are permitted to hope. That so it may be, we implore your Paternity's Benediction upon us and our mission; and I chiefly, though unworthiest of all, –

Your most Reverend Paternity's

Most humble and obedient son,

PAUL RAGUENEAU

*From the Residence of Sainte Marie,*
*among the Hurons, new France,*
*March 1, 1649.*

# IV

✳✳✳✳✳✳✳✳✳✳✳✳✳✳

A VERITABLE ACCOUNT OF THE MARTYRDOM
AND BLESSED DEATH OF FATHER JEAN DE
BREBOEUF AND OF FATHER GABRIEL
L'ALEMANT, IN NEW FRANCE,
IN THE COUNTRY OF THE
HURONS, BY THE IRO-
QUOIS, ENEMIES OF
THE FAITH

✳✳✳✳

Father Jean de Breboeuf and Father Gabriel L'Alemant[15] had set out from our cabin, to go to a small Village, called St. Ignace, distant from our cabin about a short quarter of a league, to instruct the Savages and the new Christians of that Village. It was on the 16th Day of March, in the morning, that we perceived a great fire at the place to which these two good fathers had gone. This fire made us very uneasy; we did not know whether it were enemies, or if the fire had caught in some of the huts of the village. The Reverend Father Paul Ragueneau, our Superior, immediately resolved to send someone to learn what might be the cause. But no sooner had we formed the design of going there to see, than we perceived several savages on the road, coming straight toward us. We all thought it was the Iroquois who were coming to attack us; but, having considered them more closely, we perceived that they were hurons who were fleeing from the fight, and who had escaped from the combat. These poor savages caused great pity in us. They were all covered with wounds. One had his head fractured; another his arm broken; another had an arrow in his eye; another had his hand cut off by a blow from a hatchet. In fine, the day was passed in receiving into our cabins all these poor wounded people, and in looking with compassion toward the fire, and the place where were those two good Fathers. We saw the fire and the barbarians, but we could not see anything of the two Fathers.

This is what these savages told us of the taking of the Village of St. Ignace, and about Fathers Jean de Bréboeuf and Gabriel L'Allemant:

*The Iroquois came, to the number of twelve hundred men; took our village, and seized Father Bréboeuf and his companion; and set fire to all the huts. They proceeded to vent their rage on those two Fathers, for they took them both and stripped them entirely naked, and fastened each to a post. They tied both of their hands together. They tore the nails from the fingers. They beat them with a shower of blows from cudgels, on the shoulders, the loins, the belly, the legs and the face – there being no part of their body which did not endure this torment.*

The savages told us further, that, although Father de Bréboeuf was overwhelmed under the weight of these blows, he did not cease continually to speak of God, and to encourage all the new Christians who were captives like himself to suffer well, that they might die well, in order to go in company with him to Paradise. While the good Father was thus encouraging these good people, a wretched huron renegade, – who had remained a captive with the Iroquois, and whom Father de Bréboeuf had formerly instructed and baptized, – hearing him speak of Paradise and Holy Baptism, was irritated, and said to him, "Echon," that is Father de Bréboeuf's name in Huron, "thou sayest that Baptism and the sufferings of this life lead straight to Paradise; thou wilt go soon, for I am going to baptize thee, and to make thee suffer well, in order to go the sooner to thy Paradise." The barbarian, having said that, took a kettle full of boiling water, which he poured over his body three different times, in derision of Holy baptism. And, each time that he baptized him in this manner, the barbarian said to him, with bitter sarcasm, "Go to Heaven, for thou art well baptized." After that, they made him suffer several other torments. The 1st was to make hatchets red-hot, and to apply them to the loins and under the armpits. They made a collar of these red-hot hatchets, and put it on the neck of this good Father. This is the fashion in which I have seen the collar made for other prisoners: They make six hatchets red-hot, take a large withe of green wood, pass the 6 hatchets over the large end of the withe, take the two ends together, and then put it over the neck of the sufferer. I have seen no torment which more moved me to compassion than that. For you see a man, bound naked to a post, who, having this collar on his neck, cannot tell what posture to take. For, if he lean forward, those above his shoulders weigh the more on him; if he lean back, those on his stomach make him suffer the same torment; if he keep erect, without leaning to one side or the other, the burning hatchets, applied equally on both sides, give him a double torture.

After that they put on him a belt of bark, full of pitch and resin, and set fire to it, which roasted his whole body. During all these torments, Father de Bréboeuf endured like a rock, insensible to fire and flames, which astonished all the blood-thirsty wretches who tormented him. His zeal was so great that he preached continually to these infidels, to try to convert them. His executioners were enraged against him for constantly speaking to them of God and of their conversions. To prevent him from speaking more, they cut off his tongue, and both his upper and lower lips. After that, they set themselves to strip the flesh from his legs, thighs and arms, to the very bone; and then put it to roast before his eyes, in order to eat it.

While they tormented him in this manner, those wretches derided him, saying, "Thou seest plainly that we treat thee as a friend, since we shall be the cause of thy Eternal happiness; thank us, then, for these good offices which we render thee, – for, the more thou shalt suffer, the more will thy God reward thee."

Those butchers, seeing that the good Father began to grow weak, made him sit down on the ground; and one of them, taking a knife, cut off the skin covering his skull. Another one of those barbarians, seeing that the good Father would soon die, made an opening in the upper part of his chest, and tore out his heart, which he roasted and ate. Others came to drink his blood, still warm, which they drank with both hands, – saying that Father de Bréboeuf had been very courageous to endure so much pain as they had given him, and that, by drinking his blood, they would become courageous like him.

This is what we learned of the Martyrdom and blessed death of Father Jean de Bréboeuf, by several Christian savages worthy of belief, who had been constantly present from the time the good Father was taken until his death. These good Christians were prisoners to the Iroquois, who were taking them into their country to be put to death. But our good God granted them the favor of enabling them to escape by the way; and they came to us to recount all that I have set down in writing.

Father de Bréboeuf was captured on the 16th day of March, in the morning, with Father Lalemant, in the year 1649. Father de Bréboeuf died the same day as his capture, about 4 o'clock in the afternoon. Those barbarians threw the remains of his body into the fire; but the fat which still remained on his body extinguished the fire, and he was not consumed.

I do not doubt that all I have just related is true, and I would seal it with my blood; for I have seen the same treatment given to Iroquois prisoners whom the huron savages had taken in war, with the exception of the boiling water, which I have not seen poured on any one.

I am about to describe to you truly what I saw of the Martyrdom and of the Blessed Deaths of Father Jean de Bréboeuf and of Father Gabriel L'alemant. On the next morning, when we had assurance of the departure of the enemy, we went to the spot to seek for the remains of their bodies, to the place where their lives had been taken. We found them both, but a little apart from each other. They were brought to our cabin, and laid uncovered upon the bark of trees, – where I examined them at leisure, for more than two hours, to see if what the savages had told us of their martyrdom and death were true. I examined first the Body of Father de Bréboeuf, which was pitiful to see, as well as that of Father L'alemant. Father de Bréboeuf had his legs, thighs and arms stripped of flesh to the very bone; I saw and touched a large number of great blisters, which he had on several places on his body, from the boiling water which these barbarians had poured over him in mockery of Holy Baptism. I saw and touched the wound from a belt of bark, full of pitch and resin, which roasted his whole body. I saw and touched the marks of burns from the Collar of hatchets placed on his shoulders and stomach. I saw and touched his two lips, which they had cut off because he spoke constantly of God while they made him suffer.

I saw and touched all parts of his body, which had received more than two hundred blows from a stick: I saw and touched the top of his scalped head: I saw and touched the opening which these barbarians had made to tear out his heart.

In fine, I saw and touched all the wounds of his body, as the savages had told and declared to us: we buried these precious Relics on Sunday, the 21st day of March, 1649, with much Consolation.

I had the happiness of carrying them to the grave, and of burying them with those of Father Gabriel l'alemant. When we left the country of the hurons, we raised both bodies out of the ground, and set them to boil in strong lye. All the bones were well-scraped and the care of drying them was given to me. I put them every day into a little oven which we had, made of clay, after having heated it slightly, and when in a state to be packed, they were separately enveloped in silk stuff. Then they were put into two small chests, and we brought them to Quebec, where they are held in great veneration.

It is not a Doctor of the Sorbonne who has composed this, as you may easily see; it is a relic from the Iroquois, and a person who has lived more than thought, – who is, and shall ever be, Sir,

Your Very Humble and very obedient servant,
CHRISTOPHE REGNAUT[16]

# V

✳✳✳✳✳✳✳✳✳✳✳✳✳✳✳

OF THE REMOVAL OF THE HOUSE OF SAINTE MARIE TO
THE ISLAND OF ST. JOSEPH: OF THE CAPTURE AND
DEVASTATION OF THE MISSION OF SAINT JEAN,
BY THE IROQUOIS, AND OF THE DEATH OF
FATHER CHARLES GARNIER AND OF
FATHER NOEL CHABANEL, WHO
WERE MISSIONARIES THERE

*(From the* Relation *for 1649-1650,*
*by Father Paul Ragueneau)*

✳✳✳✳

In consequence of the bloody victories obtained by the Iroquois
over our Hurons at the commencement of the spring of last
year, 1649, and of the more than inhuman acts of barbarity
practiced toward their prisoners of war, and the cruel torments
pitilessly inflicted on Father Jean de Bréboeuf and Father
Gabriel Lallemant, – terror having fallen upon the neighboring
villages, – all the inhabitants dispersed. These poor, distressed
people forsook their lands, houses, and villages, in order to
ecape the cruelty of an enemy whom they feared more than a
thousand deaths. Many, no longer expecting humanity from
man, flung themselves into the deepest recesses of the forest,
where, though it were with wild beasts, they might find peace.
Others took refuge upon some frightful rocks that lay in the
midst of a great Lake nearly four hundred leagues in circumference, – choosing rather to find death in the waters, or from
the cliffs, than by the fires of the Iroquois. A goodly number
having cast in their lot with the people of the Neutral Nation,
and with those living on the Mountain heights, whom we call

the Tobacco Nation, the most prominent of those who remained invited us to join them, rather than to flee so far away.

This was exactly what God was requiring of us, – that, in times of dire distress, we should flee with the fleeing, accompanying them everywhere; that we should lose sight of none of these Christians, although it might be expedient to detain the bulk of our forces wherever the main body of fugitives might decide to settle down.

We told off certain of our Fathers, to make some itinerant Missions, – some, in a small bark canoe, for voyaging along the coasts, and visiting the more distant islands of the great Lake, at sixty, eighty, and a hundred leagues from us; others to journey by land, making their way through forest-depths and scaling the summits of mountains.

But on each of us lay the necessity of bidding farewell to that old home of sainte Marie, – to its structures, which, though plain, seemed, in the eyes of our poor Savages, master-works of art; and to its cultivated lands, which were promising us an abundant harvest.

It was between five and six o'clock, on the evening of the fourteenth of June, that a part of our number embarked in a small vessel we had built. I, in company, with most of the others, trusted myself to some logs, fifty or sixty feet in length, which we had felled in the woods, and dragged into the water, binding all together, in order to fashion for ourselves a sort of raft that should float on that faithless element. We voyaged all night upon our great Lake, by dint of arms and oars; and we landed without mishap, after a few days, upon an island, where the Hurons were awaiting us, and which was the spot we had fixed upon for a general reunion, that we might make of it a Christian island.

The Hurons who were awaiting us on that Island, called the Island of Saint Joseph, had sown there their Indian corn; but the Summer drouths had been so excessive that they lost hope of their harvest, unless Heaven should afford them some favoring showers. On our arrival they besought us to obtain this favor for them; and our prayers were granted that very day.

These grand forests, which, since the Creation of the world, had not been felled by the hand of any man, received us as guests; while the ground furnished to us, without digging, the stone and cement we needed for fortifying ourselves against our enemies. In consequence, thank God, we found ourselves very well protected, having built a small fort according to military rules, which, therefore, could be easily defended, and would fear neither the fire, the undermining, nor the escalade of the Iroquois. . . .

In the Mountains, the people of which we name the Tobacco Nation, we have had, for some years past, two missions; in each were two of our Fathers. The one nearest to the enemy was that which bore the name of Saint Jean; its principal village, called by the same name, contained about five or six hundred families. It was a field watered by the sweat of one of the most excellent Missionaries who had dwelt in these regions, Father Charles Garnier,[17] – who was also to water it with his blood, since there both he and his flock have met death, he himself leading them even unto Paradise. . . .

It was on the seventh day of the month of last December, in the year 1649, toward three o'clock in the afternoon, that this band of Iroquois appeared at the gates of the village, spreading immediate dismay, and striking terror into all those poor people, – bereft of their strength and finding themselves vanquished; when they thought to be themselves the conquerors. Some took to flight; others were slain on the spot. To many, the flames, which were already consuming some of their cabins, gave the first intelligence of the disaster. Many were taken prisoners, but the victorious enemy, fearing the return of the warriors who had gone to meet them, hastened their retreat so precipitately, that they put to death all the old men and children, and all whom they deemed unable to keep up with them in their flight.

It was a scene of incredible cruelty. The enemy snatched from a Mother her infants, that they might be thrown into the fire; other children beheld their Mothers beaten to death at their feet, or groaning in the flames, – permission, in either case, being denied them to show the least compassion. It was a crime to shed a tear, these barbarians demanding that their prisoners should go into captivity as if they were marching to their triumph. A poor Christian Mother, who wept for the death of her infant, was killed on the spot, because she still loved, and could not stifle soon enough her Natural feelings.

Father Charles Garnier was, at that time, the only one of our

Fathers in that mission. When the enemy appeared, he was just then occupied with instructing the people in the cabins he was visiting. At the noise of the alarm, he went out, going straight to the Church, where he found some Christians. "We are dead men, my brothers," he said to them. "Pray to God, and flee by whatever way you may be able to escape. Bear about with you your faith through what of life remains; and may death find you with God in mind." He gave them his blessing, then left hurriedly, to go to the help of souls. A prey to despair, not one dreamed of defense. Several found a favorable exit for their flight; they implored the Father to flee with them, but the bonds of Charity restrained him. All unmindful of himself, he thought only of the salvation of his neighbor. Borne on by his zeal, he hastened everywhere, – either to give absolution to the Christians whom he met, or to seek, in the burning cabins, the children, the sick, or the catechumens, over whom, in the midst of the flames, he poured the waters of Holy Baptism, his own heart burning with no other fire than the love of God.

It was while thus engaged in holy work that he was encountered by the death which he had looked in the face without fearing it, or receding from it a single step. A bullet from a musket struck him, penetrating a little below the breast; another, from the same volley, tore open his stomach, lodging in the thigh, and bringing him to the ground. His courage, however, was unabated. The barbarian who had fired the shot stripped him of his cassock, and left him weltering in his blood, to pursue the other fugitives.

This good Father, a very short time after, was seen to clasp his hands, offering some prayer; then, looking about him, he perceived at a distance of ten or twelve paces, a poor dying Man, – who, like himself, had received the stroke of death, but had still some remains of life. Love of God, and zeal for Souls, were even stronger than death. Murmuring a few words of prayer, he struggled to his knees, and, rising with difficulty, dragged himself as best he might toward the sufferer, in order to assist him in dying well. He had made but three or four steps, when he fell again, somewhat heavily. Raising himself for the second time, he got, once more, upon his knees and strove to continue on his way; but his body, drained of its blood, which was flowing in abundance from his wounds, had not the strength of his courage. For the third time he fell, having proceeded but five or six steps. Further than this we have not been able to ascertain what he accomplished, – the good Christian woman who faithfully related all this to us having seen no more of him, being herself overtaken by an Iroquois, who struck her on the head with a war-hatchet, felling her upon the spot, though she afterward escaped. The Father, shortly after, received from a hatchet two blows upon the temples, one on either side, which penetrated to the brain. His body was stripped and left, entirely naked, where it lay. . . .

## OF THE DEATH OF FATHER
### NOEL CHABANEL

Here is the sixth victim whom God has taken to himself from those of our Society whom he has called to this mission of the Hurons, – there having been, as yet, not one of us who has died there without shedding his blood, and consummating the sacrifice in its entirety.

Father Noël Chabanel[18] was the Missionary companion of Father Charles Garnier; and when the village of saint Jean was taken by the Iroquois, there were but two days in which they were separated, in accordance with the orders which they had received, – our Fathers and I having thought it wiser not to keep two Missionaries exposed to danger; considering, besides, that the famine in that quarter was so severe that sufficient food for both could not be obtained. But it was not God's will that, having lived and been yoked together in the same Mission, they should be separated in death.

This good Father, then, returning whither obedience recalled him, had passed through the mission of saint Matthias, where were two others of our Fathers, and had left them on the morning of the seventh day of December. Having travelled six leagues over a most difficult road, he found himself overtaken by night in the thick of the forest, being in the company of seven or eight Christian Hurons. His men were resting, and asleep; he only was watching and in prayer. Toward midnight, he heard a noise, accompanied with cries, – partly of a victorious force who occupied that road; partly, also, of captives, taken that very day in the village of saint Jean, who were singing, as was their custom, their war-song. On hearing the noise, the Father awoke his men, who fled at once into the forest, and eventually saved themselves, – scattering, some here, some there; and taking their route toward the very place from which the enemy had come out, though a little at one side of it.

These Christians, escaped from the peril, arrived at the Tobacco Nation, and reported that the Father had gone some little way with them, intending to follow them; but that, becoming exhausted, he had fallen on his knees, saying to them, "It matters not that I die; this life is a very small consideration; of the blessedness of Paradise, the Iroquois can never rob me."

At daybreak, the Father, having altered his route, desirous of coming to the Island where we were, found himself checked at the bank of a river, which crossed his path. A Huron reported the circumstance, adding that he had passed him, in his canoe, on this side of the stream; and that, to render his flight more easy, the Father had disburdened himself of his hat, and of a bag that contained his writings; also of a blanket, which our Missionaries use as robe and cloak, as mattress and cushion, for a bed, and for every other convenience, – even for a dwelling place, when in the open country, and when they have, for a time, no other shelter. Since then we have been unable to learn any other news of the Father.

Of the manner of his death we are uncertain, – whether he may have fallen into the hands of the enemies, who actually slew on the same road some thirty persons; or that, having missed his way in the forest, he may have died there, partly from hunger, partly from cold, at the foot of some tree at which weakness obliged him to halt. But, after all, it seems to us most probable that he was murdered by that Huron, – once a Christian, but since an Apostate, – the last to see him, and who, to enjoy the possessions of the Father, would have killed him, and thrown his body into the River. Had we been inclined to pursue this matter further, I feel sure that we would have discovered proofs sufficient to convict this murderer; but, in such general misery, we judged it wiser to smother our suspicions; and we closed our own eyes to what we were well pleased was not evident. It is enough for us that God's purposes should have been served. . . .

# VI

❊❊❊❊❊❊❊❊❊❊❊❊❊❊

RELATION OF WHAT OCCURRED IN THE MISSION OF
THE FATHERS OF THE SOCIETY OF JESUS, IN THE
COUNTRY OF NEW FRANCE, FROM THE SUMMER
OF THE YEAR 1653 TO THE SUMMER OF THE
YEAR 1654

*By François-Joseph le Mercier*

❊❊❊❊

MY REVEREND FATHER:

*Pax Christi.*

I have waited until this day, the twenty-first of the month of
September, before taking my pen in hand to inform Your
Reverence of the condition in which we are, — having been
unable to do so sooner, because we did not know it ourselves.
Our minds have been so divided during the past year that, to tell
the truth, we have enjoyed Peace while thinking we were at war.
Therein God has blessed our administration; and from the plots
of treachery entertained by the Iroquois, our enemies, he has
derived their welfare and ours. Such are the hopes given us in
this matter by the fortunate results of a journey which one of
our Fathers has recently made to that country. It was Father
Simon le Moine,[19] who was sent thither in the beginning of July,
and left us in suspense until his return, a few days ago, at which
we were filled with a joy that was all the greater as we had
reason to fear that he had been cruelly burnt, — which fate has
already befallen several of our Fathers at the hands of these
wretches. But God guided all the Father's steps in the heart of
the Iroquois Nation. He found there a captive Church, composed of our old time Hurons. He converted a great Iroquois

Captain, the Chief of eighteen hundred men, whom he was leading to a new war. Finally the Father received presents from the most important nation; it is centrally situated among the other Iroquois nations, who are inviting us to go and instruct them. We gave them our word that next Spring we would go and dwell there, building a house like the one we used to have among the Hurons before the war had driven us thence.

The enterprise of establishing a Mission next Spring in the heart of the Iroquois Nation obliges us to ask Your Reverence for the aid of six of our Fathers, for we are too few. Monsieur de Lauson, our Governor, intends to send thither a number of picked Frenchmen for starting a new settlement; while we shall send some of our Fathers and some workmen to build the first Church there in honor of the most Blessed Virgin. The expense will be excessive; but as it is an affair of God more than ours, his Providence will provide for it. Even if we should be obliged to set out, as we often did in our Huron missions, with only a staff in hand, and only our trust in God for maintenance, Our Fathers are all resolved to make the attempt. There will be a great deal to do, and much more to suffer, and everything to fear; for we have to deal with Barbarous Nations, who breathe only blood and have drunk that of the Martyrs.

## JOURNEY OF FATHER SIMON LE MOINE
## TO THE COUNTRY OF THE IROQUOIS,
### IN JULY, AUGUST, AND SEPTEMBER

On the second days of the month of July (1654), Father Simon le Moine set out from Quebec on his journey to the Onnon-taehronnon Iroquois [Onondagas]. Passing by three Rivers, he proceded thence to Montreal, where a young man of stout heart and long a resident here, very piously joined him. For greater ease I will follow the Father's journal. . . .

*At each of my presents they uttered a loud shout of applause from the depths of their chests, in evidence of their delight. I was occupied fully two hours in delivering my entire harangue, which I pronounced in the tone of a Captain, – walking back and forth, as is their custom, like an actor on a stage.*

*After that they gathered together by Nations and bands, calling to them an Anniehronnon [Mohawk] who by good luck happened to be present. They consulted together for more than two hours longer, when they at length called me back and gave me a seat of honor among them.*

*That one of the Captains who is the tongue of the Country and acts as its orator, repeated faithfully the substance of all that I had said. Then they all began to sing to express their joy; and told me that I might, for my part, pray to God, which I did very willingly. . . .*

*To conclude these thanksgivings, the Onnontaerrhonnon Captain took the word. "Listen, Ondessonk," he said to me: "Five whole Nations address thee through my mouth; I have in my heart the sentiments of all the Iroquois Nations, and my tongue is faithful to my heart. Thou shalt tell Onnontio [the* governor of New France] *four things, which are the gist of all our deliberations in Council.*

*"1. It is our wish to acknowledge him of whom thou has told us, who is the master of our lives, and who is unknown to us.*

*"2. The May-tree for all matters of concern to us is to-day planted at Onnontagué." He meant that that would be thenceforth the scene of the assemblies and parleys relating to the Peace.*

*"3. We conjure you to choose a site that will be advantageous to yourselves, on the shores of our great lake, in order to build thereon a French settlement. Place yourselves in the heart of the country, since you are to possess our hearts. Thither we will go to receive instruction, and thence you will be able to spread out in all directions. Show us Paternal care, and we will render you filial obedience.*

*"4. We are involved in new wars, wherein Onnontio gives us courage; but for him we shall have only thoughts of Peace."*

*They had reserved their richest presents to accompany these last four words; but I am sure that their countenances spoke more eloquently than their tongues, and joy was depicted on their faces, with so much kindness that my heart was deeply moved.*

*On the eleventh day of August, there was nothing but feasting and rejoicing on every hand. At night, however, a disaster befell us: a cabin having caught fire, – we know not how, – a furious wind carried the flames to the others; and in less than two hours more than twenty of them were reduced to ashes, while the rest of the village was in danger of destruction. Nevertheless, God maintained the spirits of all in the joy of the preceding day, and kept their hearts as calm toward me as if this misfortune had not occurred. . . .*

# VII

JOURNEY OF FATHERS JOSEPH CHAUMONT
AND CLAUDE DABLON TO ONONTAGUE, A
COUNTRY OF THE UPPER IROQUOIS[20]

*(From the* Relation *for 1655-56)*

✳✳✳✳

The people named Agneronnons are called the Iroquois of the
lowlands, or the Lower Iroquois; while we speak of the Onon-
taeronons, and other Nations near these, as the Iroquois of the
highlands, or the Upper Iroquois, because they are situated
nearer the source of the great Saint Lawrence river and inhabit
a country full of mountains. Onontaé – or as others pronounce
it, Onontagué – is the chief town of the Onontaeronnons; and
thither our course was directed. . . .

All the first day was spent, partly in feasting, partly in nego-
tiating peace for the Algonquins; and, as this was the most
difficult matter, it demanded the most serious deliberation. . . .

To show his joy over this glory, the Deputy [from the
Mohawk tribe] began a song, which was as pleasing as it was
new. All present sang with him, but in a different and heavier
tone, beating time on their mats; while the man himself danced
in the midst of them all, performing strange antics, – keeping
his whole body in motion; making gestures with his hands, feet,
head, eyes and mouth, – and all this so exactly in the time of
both his own singing and that of the others, that the result was
admirable. He sang these words: *A, a, ha, Gaianderé, gaianderé*;
that is, translated into Latin, *Io, io, triumphe.* And then, *E, e, he,
Gaianderé, gaianderé; O, o, ho, Gaianderé, gaianderé.* He explained what he meant by his *Gaianderé*, which signifies, among
the natives, "something very excellent." He said that, what we

call the Faith, would be called by them *Gaianderé*; and, to explain it better, he offered his first piece of porcelain.

He offered the second in behalf of the Onneioutchronnon [Oneidas], because as they were both twin brothers, he thought that he, too, ought to thank Onnontio, since he shared the happiness of being adopted by him.

The third was an assurance that the present offered by us the day before, to unite the minds of the Anniehronnons with those of the four other Nations, would be effectual.

The fourth pleased us greatly, being given in declaration that not only the Father, but also his two children, would all become sincere believers, – meaning, that both the Onnontagueronnon [Onondagas], who is the father, and the Oiogeon and Onneiout [Cayugas and Oneidas], who are his children, would embrace the Faith.

With the fifth, he adopted the Hurons and Algonquins as his brothers; and with the sixth, promised that the three Nations should unite, and go, the following Spring, to bring the French and the Savages who should desire to come into their Country.

It was necessary to make a reply to all of this, which the Father did in two words, each accompanied by a present. One was to repair the rents made in our Cabin by the people who crowded it every day, and who could not see their fill of us; and the other was to clean the mat on which future Councils between their Country and the French and their Allies were to be held.

This beautiful day closed with the teaching of a score of people of the Village, who presented themselves anew in order to pray. . . .

# VIII

✴✴✴✴✴✴✴✴✴✴✴✴✴

LETTER TO REVEREND FATHER LOUYS CELLOT,
PROVINCIAL OF THE SOCIETY OF JESUS IN
THE PROVINCE OF FRANCE, BY FATHER
FRANÇOIS-JOSEPH LE MERCIER
(1656)

✴✴✴✴

MY REVEREND FATHER:

*Pax Christi:*

. . . . The manifestations of Divine providence and the means
employed by its guidance, which has so well directed matters to
the point at which they have now arrived, compel us to admit
that we cannot, without extreme cowardice, disappoint the
expectations that God has caused to arise for us where we least
expected them. For what power other than his could force these
peoples [the Iroquois], inflated with pride on account of their
victories, not only to come and seek a peace with us of which
they seem to have no need, but also to place themselves unarmed
in our hands, and throw themselves at our feet, – begging us to
accept them as our friends, when we were so weak that we could
no longer withstand them as enemies? They had but to continue,
to massacre the remainder of the French Colony, for they met
with hardly any resistance, either from the French or from the
Savages, our Confederates; and nevertheless, for over three
years, they incessantly sent presents and embassies to ingratiate
themselves with us, and to solicit us to make peace. Old and
young, women and children, place themselves at our mercy;
they enter our forts; they act confidently with us, and spare no
effort to open their hearts to us, and to make us read therein
that all their solicitations are as sincere as they are pressing.

They are not content with coming to us, but for a long time they invited us to go to them, and offer us the finest land that they have, and that is to be found in this New world. Neither the necessities of trade nor the hopes of our protection induce them to do all that; for they have hitherto had and still enjoy both those things with the Dutch, much more advantageously than they can ever hope to do with the French. But it is the act of God; he has, doubtless, lent an ear to the blood of the Martyrs, which is the seed of Christians, and which now causes them to spring up in this land that was watered by it. . . .

Divine providence also manifests itself by giving us at this moment a goodly number of our Fathers, who not only have the courage to expose themselves to everything, but also possess the capacity of teaching these Barbarians, – whose language, as well as that of many other Nations still more remote, is not very different from that of the Hurons. It is this that revives their fervor and gives to old men, broken down after glorious labors, the courage to desire to go among those peoples, and to spend the remainder of their lives, with the same zeal that they manifested fifteen or twenty years ago when they labored in the Huron Missions.

It is true that the stumbling-block which might hinder our design lies with the lower Iroquois, called Anniengehronnons [Mohawks],with whom we do not go to dwell. They may presume that, if we unite ourselves so closely with the four Upper Nations, it will be to place ourselves in a position to fear them no longer. But, even if they should oppose our establishment, we far prefer to have them alone for enemies than the Four Nations together; these would become irritated if we refused them our friendship, and – seeing themselves disappointed in their just expectations, and so manifestly deceived after such solemn promises, so frequently reiterated both here and in their country, to go and settle their land – that they would make us experience the baleful effects of that vexation. Thus, a refusal or delay would be followed by the total ruin of this New France, which, after being reduced to extremities by a single Nation, could not long withstand the efforts of five together, if they conspired against her. The blessing of peace, which we are beginning to enjoy, is so sweet and so necessary for the publication of the Faith that, even if there were great danger, we would willingly immolate ourselves, as public victims, to avert the storm which would inevitably burst upon our French, and to ward off the misfortunes which would accompany a war more dangerous than those that preceded it. . . .

And, for my part, I beg Your Reverence and all our Fathers and Brethren of your Province to lift your hands to heaven, while we go to declare war against Infidelity, and to fight the Devil in the very heart of his country. I am, with all possible respect and submission,

Your Reverence's

Very humble and very obedient

servant in Our Lord,

FRANCOIS LE MERCIER,

of the Society of Jesus.

*From Montreal, this*
*6th of June, 1656.*

# IX

❋❋❋❋❋❋❋❋❋❋❋❋❋❋

## LETTER OF FATHER CLAUDE CHAUCHETIERE,[21] RESPECTING THE IROQUOIS MISSION OF SAULT ST. FRANCOIS XAVIER, NEAR MONTREAL

*Sault St. François Xavier,*
*this 14th of October, 1682.*

❋❋❋

MY REVEREND FATHER:

*Pax Christi:*

In answer to Your Reverence's letter respecting what you have asked me, I will say that we are in a part of the country where the climate is not as good as in france, although, thanks be to God, I am in very good health. We are in a very high and beautiful location, with a fine view, 60 leagues Distant from Quebec, – which is called "the Iroquois mission." It is the finest mission in Canada, and, as regards piety and devotion, resembles one of the best churches in France. . . .

We have a large farm, on which we keep oxen, cows, and poultry, and gather corn for our subsistance. It is sometimes necessary to take charge of all temporal as well as spiritual matters, now that Father Fremin has gone down in an Infirm condition to Quebec, as well as Father Cholenec. Some savages get their land Plowed, and harvest french wheat, Instead of Indian corn. It is impossible to describe their Joy when They can harvest 20 or 30 minots [22 or 33 bushels] of french wheat, and are able to eat bread from time to time. But as this sort of grain costs them too much labor, their usual occupation is to Plow the soil in order to plant indian corn in it. If The Savages were fed, they would work much more than they do. . . .

You will be pleased to hear from me respecting the austerities practised by certain savage women – Although there may be some indiscretion in their doing so; but it will show you their fervor. More than 5 years ago some of them learned, I know not how, of the pious practises followed by the nuns in Montreal who are hospital sisters. They heard of disciplines, of iron girdles, and of hair shirts. This religious life began to please them very much, and three of them formed an association, in order to commence a sort of Convent; but we stopped them, because we did not Think that The time had come for this. However, even if they were not cloistered, they at least observed Chastity; and one of them died with the reputation of sanctity, 3 years Ago next spring. They, and some others who imitated them, would be admired in france, if what they do were known there.

The first who began made her first attempt about Christmas in The year 1676, when she divested herself of her clothing, and exposed herself to The air at the foot of a large Cross that stands beside our Cemetery. She did so at a time when the snow was falling, although she was pregnant; and the snow that fell upon her back caused her so much suffering that she nearly died from it – as well as her child, whom the cold chilled in its mother's womb. It was her own idea to do this – to do penance for her sins, she said. She has had four companions in her fervor, who have since imitated her. Two of them made a hole in the ice, in the depth of winter, and Threw themselves into The water, where they remained during the time that it would take to say a Rosary slowly and sedately. One of the two, who Feared that she would be found out, did not venture to Warm herself when she returned to her cabin, but lay down on her mat with lumps of ice adhering to her shoulders. There have been several other Inventions of similar mortifications, which men and women have discovered for the purpose of tormenting themselves, and which constitute their usual penance. But we have made them give up whatever was excessive. . . .

# PART FOUR

✳✳✳✳

# THE WESTERN MISSIONS AND THE EXPANSION OF NEW FRANCE

✳✳✳✳✳✳✳✳✳✳✳✳✳✳✳

# I

✳✳✳✳✳✳✳✳✳✳✳✳✳✳✳

## OF THE CONDITION OF THE COUNTRY IN GENERAL

(*From the* Relation *for 1659-60, written by Father Jérôme Lalemant.*)

✳✳✳✳

We know that very far beyond the great lake of the Hurons — when the Iroquois did not molest our mission, and before he had expelled us from them by the murder of our Fathers, — we know that some remnants of the wreck of that Nation rallied in considerable numbers beyond the lakes and mountains frequented by their enemies, and that but recently they sent a deputation hither to ask back again their dear old Pastors. But these good pastors are slain on the way, by the Iroquois, their guides are captured and burned, and all the roads are rendered impossible.

We even know that among the Iroquois the Faith is in a vigorous condition, although they do not possess it in their own persons, but in those of numerous captives. These only long to have us with them, or to be themselves with us. Finally we know that, whithersoever we go in the forests, we find some fugitive Church, or else some infant one; everywhere we find children to send to heaven, and adults to instruct; but everywhere, too, we find the Iroquois, who, like an obtrusive phantom, besets us in all places. They prevent the tribes from five or six hundred leagues about us from coming down hither, laden with furs that would make this country overflow with immense riches — as was done in a single journey which some of those Nations undertook this year — although secretly, and, as it were, by stealth, from fear of their foes.

What gives the enemy this advantage over us is, that all the rural settlements outside Quebec are without defense, and are distant from one another as much as eight or ten leagues on the banks of the great river. In each house there are only two, three, or four men, and often only one, alone with his wife and a number of children, who may all be killed or carried off without anyone's knowing aught about it in the nearest house. They come like Foxes through the woods. They attack like lions. They take flight like birds, disappearing before they have really appeared.

I say nothing of the losses that France would suffer if these vast regions should pass from her control. The foreigner would reap a great advantage, to the detriment of French navigation. . . .

But what is more astonishing is, that they actually hold dominion for five hundred leagues around, although their numbers are very small; for, of the five Nations constituting the Iroquois, the Agnieronnons do not exceed five hundred men able to bear arms, who occupy three or four wretched Villages.

It is beyond doubt that, if the Anieronnons were defeated by the French, the other Iroquois Nations would be glad to compromise with us. Then those fair Missions would be revived at Onnontagué, at Oiogoen, and in all the other remaining Iroquois Nations, where we have already sown the first seeds of the faith. Moreover the great door would be open toward the tribes of the North, and toward those newly discovered ones of the West, all of whom we embrace under the general name of Algonkins. . . .

## OF THE CONDITION OF THE ALGONKIN
## COUNTRY, AND OF SOME NEW
### DISCOVERIES

I cannot more clearly describe the condition of the Nations of the Algonkin tongue than by giving the simple account of what one of our Fathers has learned about them, – who has been, this year, on the Saguenay River of Tadoussac, – as Providence gave him opportunities for this during that journey.

*On the thirtieth of July of the year one thousand six hundred and sixty, ascending the Saguené to the distance of thirty-two leagues from Tadoussac, I encountered eighty Savages; and among them was one named Awatanik, a man of importance because he was a Captain in rank, and much more so because he had received holy Baptism ten years before in the country of the Nipisiriniens. . . .*

He started, in the month of June of the year one thousand six hundred and fifty-eight, from the lake of the Ouinipegouek [Lake Nipissing], which is strictly only a large bay in lake Huron. It is called by others "the lake of the stinkards," not because it is salt, like the water of the Sea, – which the Savages call Ouinipeg, or "stinking water," – but because it is surrounded by sulphurous soil, whence issue several springs which convey into this lake the impurities absorbed by their waters in the places of their origin.

He passed the remainder of that summer and the following winter near the lake which we call Superior, from its position above that of the Hurons, into which it empties by a water fall that has also given it its name; and, as our traveler halted there for some time, let us pause a while with him to note the peculiarities of the place.

This lake, which is more than eighty leagues long by forty wide in certain places, is studded with Islands picturesquely distributed along its shores. The whole length of its coast is lined with Algonkin Nations, fear of the Iroquois having forced them to seek there an asylum. It is also enriched in its entire circumference with mines of lead in a nearly pure state; with copper of such excellence that pieces as large as one's fist are found, all refined; and with great rocks, having whole veins of turquoise [amethyst]. *The people even strive to make us believe that its waters are swollen by various streams which roll along with the sand grains of gold in abundance – the refuse, so to speak, of the neighboring mines. What inclines us to believe this, is that, when the foundations of saint Joseph's Chapel were dug on the shore of Lake Huron, – which is nothing but the discharge of lake Superior, – the workmen found a vein, as large as one's arm, of these grains of gold, the sand that was mixed with the vein being so little in quantity as to be almost imperceptible in comparison with the rest. . . .*

*Now we know that, proceeding Southward for about three hundred leagues from the end of the lake Superior, of which I have just spoken, we come to the bay of St. Esprit* [Mobile Bay?], *which lies on the thirtieth degree of latitude and the two hundred and eightieth of longitude, in the Gulf of Mexico, on the coast of Florida; and in a Southwesternly direction from the same extremity of lake Superior, it is about two hundred leagues to another lake, which empties into the Vermilion sea on the coast of New Grenada* [California], *in the great South Sea. It is from one of these two coasts that the Savages who live some sixty leagues to the West of our lake Superior obtain European goods, and they even say that they have seen some Europeans there.*

*Moreover, from this same lake Superior, following a River toward the North, we arrive, after eight or ten days' journey, at Hudson Bay, in fifty-five degrees of latitude. From this place, in a Northwesterly direction, it is about forty leagues by land to Button Bay, where lies port Melson;*[22] *on the fifty-seventh degree of latitude and the two hundred and seventieth of longitude; the distance thence to Japan is to be reckoned at only one thousand four hundred and twenty leagues, there being only seventy-one degrees of a great circle intervening. These two Seas, then, of the South and of the North, being known, there remains only that of the West, which joins them, to make only one from the three; and it is the fresh knowledge that we have gained from a Nation which, being situated at about the forty-seventh degree of latitude and the two hundred and seventy-third of longitude, assures us that ten days' journey Westward lies the Sea, which can be no other than the one we are looking for, – it is this knowledge that makes us believe that the whole of North America, being thus surrounded by the sea on the east, South, West and North, must be separated from Groeslande [Greenland] by some strait, of which a good part has already been discovered; and that it only remains now to push on some degrees farther, to enter nothing less than the Japan sea. In order to make the passage of Hudson strait, this is to be attempted only in the months of August and September; for during these months only, the passage is less blocked with ice.*

*But enough for the present. If the Iroquois permit, we shall be fully able to go and enlighten ourselves more clearly concerning this discovery, which, being known to us only through the medium of Savages, does not give us all the information we might desire. . . .*

*But if the Iroquois goes thither, why shall not we also? If there are conquests to make, why shall not the faith make them, since it makes them in all parts of the world?*

# II

✳✳✳✳✳✳✳✳✳✳✳✳✳✳

JOURNAL OF FATHER CLAUDE
ALLOUEZ'S VOYAGE INTO
THE OUTAOUAC
COUNTRY

(*From the* Relation *for 1666-67,
written by Father François-
Joseph le Mercier*)

✳✳✳✳

Two years ago and more, Father Claude Allouez[23] set out for that great and arduous Mission, in behalf of which he has journeyed, in all his travels, nearly two thousand leagues through these vast forests, — enduring hunger, nakedness, shipwreck, weariness by day and night, and the persecution of the Idolators; but he has also had the consolation of bearing the torch of the faith to more than twenty different infidel Nations.

We cannot gain a better knowledge of the fruits of his labors than from the Journal which he was called upon to prepare. He begins as follows:

*On the eighth of August, in the year 1665, I embarked at three Rivers with six Frenchmen, in company with more than four hundred Savages of various nations, who, after transacting the little trading for which they had come, were returning to their own country.*

*The Devil offered all conceivable opposition to our journey, making use of the false prejudice held by these savages, that Baptism causes their children to die. . . .*

*Toward the beginning of September, after coasting along the shores of the Lake of the Hurons, we reached the Sault; for such is the name given to a half-league of rapids that are encountered in a beautiful river which unites two great Lakes – that of the Hurons, and Lake Superior.*

*This River is pleasing, not only on account of the Islands intercepting its course and the great bays bordering it, but because of the fishing and hunting, which are excellent there. We sought a resting place for the night on one of these Islands, where our Savages thought they would find provision for supper upon their arrival; for, as soon as they had landed, they put the kettle on the fire, expecting to see the Canoe laden with fish the moment the net was cast into the water! But God chose to punish their presumption, and deferred giving any food to the starving men until the following day.*

*On the second of September, then, after clearing this Sault, – which is not a waterfall, but merely a very swift current impeded by numerous rocks, – we entered Lake Superior, which will henceforth bear Monsieur de Tracy's*[24] *name, in recognition of indebtedness to him on the part of the people of those regions.*

*The form of this lake is nearly that of a bow, the Southern shore being much curved and the Northern nearly straight. Fish are abundant there, and of excellent quality; while the water is so clear and pure that objects at the bottom can be seen to the depth of six brasses.*

*One often finds at the bottom of the water pieces of pure copper, of ten and twenty livres' weight. I have several times seen such pieces in the Savages hands; and since they are superstitious, they keep them as so many divinities, or as presents which the gods dwelling beneath the water have given them, and on which their welfare is to depend. For this reason they preserve these pieces of copper, wrapped up, among their most precious possessions. Some have kept them for more than fifty years; others have had them in their families from time immemorial, and cherish them as household gods.*

*For some time, there had been a sort of great rock, all of copper, the point of which projected from the water; this gave the passers-by the opportunity to go and cut off pieces from it. When, however, I passed that spot, nothing more was seen of it; and I think that the storms – which here are very frequent, and like those at sea – have covered the rock with sand. Our Savages tried to persuade me that it was a divinity, who had disappeared for some reason they do not state.*

*This Lake is, furthermore, the resort of twelve or fifteen distinct nations – coming, some from the North, others from the South, and still others from the West; and they all betake themselves either to the best parts of the shore for fishing, or to the Islands, which are scattered in great numbers all over the Lake. These peoples' motive in repairing hither is partly to obtain food by fishing, and partly to transact their petty trading with one another, when they meet. But God's purpose was to facilitate the proclaiming of the Gospel to wandering and vagrant tribes – as will appear in the course of this Journal.*

*Having, then, entered Lake Tracy, we spent the whole month of September in coasting along its southern shore – where, finding myself alone with our Frenchmen, I had the consolation of saying holy Mass, which I had been unable to do since my departure from three Rivers.*

*We then crossed the Bay named for Saint Theresa by the late Father Menard.[25] There this brave missionary spent a winter, laboring with the same zeal which afterward made him sacrifice his life in quest for souls. I found, at no great distance thence, some remnants of his labors, in the persons of two Christian women who had always kept the faith, and who shone like two stars amid the darkness of that infidelity. I made them pray to God, after I had refreshed their memory concerning our mysteries.*

# III

## TAKING POSSESSION, IN THE KING'S NAME OF ALL THE COUNTRIES COMMONLY INCLUDED UNDER THE DESIGNATION OUTAOUAC

*(From the* Relation *for 1671-72, by Father Claude Dablon)*

✳✳✳✳

It is well to afford a general view of all these Outaouac territories, not only for the purpose of designating the places where the Faith has been proclaimed by the planting of Missions, but also because the King, by very recently taking possession of them with a ceremony worthy of the eldest son of the Church, put all these tribes under the protection of the Cross before receiving them under his own — as will be set forth in the account to be given of that act of taking possession.

By glancing, as one can, at the Map of the lakes, and of the territories on which are settled most of the tribes of these regions, one will gain more light upon all these Missions than by long descriptions that might be given of them.

The reader may first turn his eyes to the Mission of Sainte Marie du Sault, three leagues below the mouth of Lake superior. He will find it situated on the banks of the river by which this great Lake discharges its waters, at the place called the Sault, very advantageous in which to perform Apostolic functions, since it is the great resort of most of the Savages of these regions, and lies in the almost universal route of all who go down to the French settlements. It was also on this spot that all these lands were taken possession of in his Majesty's name, in the presence and with the approval of fourteen Nations who had come hither for that purpose. . . .

When Monsieur Talon, our Intendant, returned from Portugal, and after his shipwreck, he was commanded by the King to return to this country; and at the same time received his Majesty's orders to exert himself strenuously for the establishment of Christianity here, by aiding our Missions, and to cause the name and the sovereignty of our invincible Monarch to be acknowledged by even the least known and the most remote Nations. These commands, reinforced by the designs of the Minister [Colbert], – who is ever equally alert to extend God's glory, and to promote that of his King in every land, – were obeyed as speedily as possible. Monsieur Talon had no sooner landed than he considered means for insuring the success of these plans, – choosing to that end sieur de saint Lusson, whom he commissioned to take possession, in his place and in his Majesty's name, of the territories lying between the East and the West, from Montreal as far as the South sea, covering the utmost extent and range possible.

For this purpose, after wintering on the Lake of the Hurons, Monsieur de saint Lusson repaired to sainte Marie du Sault early in May of this year, sixteen hundred and seventy-one. First, he summoned the surrounding tribes living within a radius of a hundred leagues, and even more; and they responded through their Ambassadors, to the number of fourteen Nations. After making all necessary preparations for the successful issue of the whole undertaking to the honor of France, he began, on June fourth of the same year, with the most solemn ceremony ever observed in these regions.

For, when all had assembled in a great public council, and a height had been chosen well adapted to his purpose, – overlooking, as it did, the Village of the people of the Sault, – he caused the Cross to be planted there, and then the King's standard to be raised, with all the pomp that he could devise.

The Cross was publicly blessed, with all the ceremonies of the Church, by the Superior of these Missions; and then, when it had been raised from the ground for the purpose of planting it, the *Vexilla* was sung. Many Frenchmen there present at the time joined in this hymn, to the wonder and delight of the assembled Savages; while the whole company was filled with a common joy at the sight of this glorious standard of JESUS

CHRIST, which seemed to have been raised so high only to rule over the hearts of all these poor peoples.

Then the French Escutcheon, fixed to a Cedar pole, was also erected, above the Cross, while the *Exaudiat* was sung, and prayer for his Majesty's Sacred person was offered in that faraway corner of the world. After this, Monsieur de saint Lusson, observing all the forms customary on such occasions, took possession of those regions, while the air resounded with repeated shouts of "Long live the King!" and with the discharge of musketry, – to the delight and astonishment of all those people, who had never seen anything of the kind.

After this confused uproar of voices and muskets had ceased, perfect silence was imposed upon the whole assemblage; and Father Claude Allouez began to Eulogize the King, in order to make all those Nations understand what sort of a man he was whose standard they beheld, and to whose sovereignty they were that day submitting. Being well versed in their tongue and in their ways, he was so successful in adapting himself to their comprehension as to give them such an opinion of our incomparable Monarch's greatness that they have no words with which to express their thoughts upon the subject. . . .

# IV

✻✻✻✻✻✻✻✻✻✻✻✻✻✻

OF THE FIRST VOYAGE MADE BY FATHER
MARQUETTE TOWARD NEW MEXICO,
AND HOW THE IDEA THEREOF
WAS CONCEIVED
(1673)

(*From the preface to Marquette's Journal, written
by Father Claude Dablon*)

✻✻✻✻

The Father[26] had long premeditated This Undertaking, influenced by a most ardent desire to extend the Kingdom of Jesus Christ, and to make him Known and adored by all the peoples of that country. He saw himself, As it were, at the door of these new Nations when, as early as the year 1670, he was laboring in the Mission at the point of st. Esprit, at the extremity of lake superior, among the outaouacs; he even saw occasionally various persons belonging to these new peoples from whom he obtained all the Information that he could. This induced him to make several efforts to commence this undertaking, but ever in vain; and he even lost all hope of succeeding therein, when God brought about for him the following opportunity.

In the year 1673, Monsieur The Count De Frontenac, Our Governor, and Monsieur Talon, then our Intendant, Recognizing the Importance of this discovery, — either that they might seek a passage from there to the sea of China, by the river that discharges into the Vermillion, or California Sea; or because they desired to verify what has for some time been said concerning the 2 Kingdoms of Theguaio And Quiuira,[27] which Border on Canada, and in which numerous gold mines are reported to exist, — these Gentlemen, I say, appointed at the same time for

This undertaking Sieur Jolyet, whom they considered very fit for so great an enterprise; and they were well pleased that Father Marquette should be of the party.

They were not mistaken in the choice they made of Sieur Jolyet, For he is a young man, born in this country, who possesses all the qualifications that could be desired for such an undertaking. He has experience and Knows the Languages spoken in the country of the Outaouacs, where he has passed several years. He possesses Tact and prudence, which are the chief qualities necessary for the success of a voyage as dangerous as it is difficult. Finally, he has the Courage to dread nothing where everything is to be Feared. Consequently, he has fulfilled all The expectations entertained of him; and if, having passed through a thousand dangers, he had not unfortunately been wrecked in the very harbor, his Canoe having been upset below sault st Louys, near Montreal, – where he lost both his men and his papers, and whence he escaped only by a sort of Miracle, – nothing would have been left to be desired in the success of his Voyage.

## THE JOURNAL OF FATHER
### JACQUES MARQUETTE

. . . . Accordingly, on the 17th day of may, 1673, we started from the Mission of st. Ignace at Michilimakinac, where I Then was. The Joy that we felt at being selected for This Expedition animated our Courage, and rendered the labor of paddling from morning to night agreeable to us. And because We were going to seek Unknown countries, we took every precaution in our power, so that, if our Undertaking were hazardous, it should not be foolhardy. . . .

The first Nation that we came to was That of the folle avoine [Menomenees]. I entered Their River, to go and visit these peoples to whom we have preached The Gospel for several years, – in consequence of which, there are several good christians among Them. . . .

I told these peoples of the folle avoine of My design to go and discover Those Remote nations, in order to Teach them the Mysteries of Our Holy Religion. They were Greatly surprised to hear it, and did their best to dissuade me. They represented to me that I would meet Nations who never show mercy to Strangers, but Break Their heads without any cause; and that war was kindled Between Various peoples who dwelt upon our Route, which Exposed us to the further manifest danger of being killed by the bands of Warriors who are ever in the Field. They also said that the great River was very dangerous, when one does not know the difficult Places; that it was full of horrible monsters, which devoured men and Canoes Together; that there was even a demon, who was heard from a great distance, who barred the way, and swallowed up all who ventured to approach him; Finally that the Heat was so excessive In those countries that it would Inevitably Cause Our death.

I thanked them for the good advice that they gave me, but told them that I could not follow it, because the salvation of souls was at stake, for which I would be delighted to give my life; that I scoffed at the alleged demon; that we would easily defend ourselves against those marine monsters; and, moreover, that We would be on our guard to avoid the other dangers with which they threatened us. After making them pray to God, and giving them some Instruction, I separated from them. . . .

Here we are at Maskoutens. This Word may, in Algonquin, mean, "the fire Nation," – which, indeed, is the name given to this tribe. Here is the limit of the discoveries which the french have made, For they have not yet gone any further.

This Village Consists of three Nations who have gathered there – Miamis, Maskoutens, and Kikabous. The former are the most civil, the most liberal, and the most shapely. They wear two long locks over their ears, which give them a pleasing appearance. They are regarded as warriors, and rarely undertake expeditions without being successful. They are very docile, and listen quietly to What is said to Them; and they appeared so eager to Hear Father Alloues when he Instructed them that they gave Him but little rest, even during the night. The Maskoutens and Kikabous are ruder, and seem peasants in comparison with the others. As Bark for making Cabins is scarce in this country They use Rushes; these serve Them for making walls and Roofs, but do not afford them much protection against the winds, and still less against the rains when they fall abundantly. The Advantage of Cabins of this kind is, that they make packages of Them, and easily transport them wherever they wish, while they are hunting. . . .

We knew that, at three leagues from Maskoutens, was a River, which discharged into Missisipi. We knew also that the direction we were to follow in order to reach it was west-southwesterly. But the road is broken by so many swamps and small lakes that it is easy to lose one's way, especially as the [Fox] River leading thither is so full of wild oats that it is difficult to find the Channel. For this reason we greatly needed our two guides, who safely Conducted us to a portage of 2,700 paces, and helped us to transport our Canoes to enter That river; after which they returned home, leaving us alone in this Unknown county, in the hands of providence.

Thus we left the Waters flowing to Quebec, 4 or 500 Leagues from here, to float on Those that would thenceforward Take us through strange lands. Before embarking thereon, we Began all together a new devotion to the blessed Virgin Immaculate, which we practised daily, addressing to her special prayers to place under her protection both our persons and the success of our voyage; and, after mutually encouraging one another, we entered our Canoes.

The River on which we embarked is called Meskousing [Wisconsin]. It is very wide; it has a sandy bottom, which forms various shoals that render its navigation very difficult. It is full of Islands Covered with Vines. On the banks one sees fertile land, diversified with woods, prairies, and Hills. There are oak, Walnut and basswood trees; and another kind, whose branches are armed with long thorns. We saw there neither feathered game nor fish, but many deer and a large number of cattle [bison]. Our Route lay to the southwest, and, after navigating about 30 leagues, we saw a spot presenting all the appearances of an iron mine; and, in fact, one of our party who had formerly seen such mines, assures us that The One which We found is very good and very rich. It is Covered with three feet of good soil, and is quite near a chain of rocks, the base of which is covered by very fine trees. After proceeding 40 leagues on This same route, we arrived at the mouth of our River, and, at 42 and a half degrees of latitude, We safely entered Missisipi on the 17th of June, with a Joy that I cannot Express. . . .

## OF THE CHARACTER OF THE ILINOIS;
## OF THEIR HABITS AND CUSTOMS

When one speaks the word "Ilinois" it is as if one said in their language, "the men," – As if the other Savages were looked upon by them merely as animals. It must also be admitted that they have an air of humanity which we have not observed in the other nations that we have seen upon our route. The shortness Of my stay among Them did not allow me to secure all the Information that I would have desired; among all Their customs, the following is what I have observed.

They are divided into many villages, some of which are quite distant from that of which we speak, which is called peouarea. This causes some difference in their language, which, on the whole, resembles allegonquin, so that we easily understood each other. They are of a gentle and tractable disposition; we Experienced this in the reception which they gave us. They have several wives, of whom they are Extremely jealous; they watch them very closely, and cut off their noses or ears when they misbehave. I saw several women who bore the marks of their misconduct. Their Bodies are shapely; they are active and very skillful with their bows and arrows. They also use guns, which they buy from our savage allies who Trade with our french. They use them especially to inspire, through their noise and smoke, terror in their Enemies; the latter do not use guns, and have never seen any, since they live too Far toward the West. They are warlike, and make themselves dreaded by the Distant tribes to the south and west, whither they go to procure Slaves; these they barter, selling them at a high price to other Nations, in exchange for other Wares. Those very Distant Savages against whom they war, have no Knowledge of Europeans; neither do they know anything of iron, or of Copper, and they have only stone Knives. When the Ilinois depart to go to war, the whole village must be notified by a loud Shout, which is uttered at the doors of their Cabins, the night and The Morning before their departure. The Captains are distinguished from the warriors by wearing red Scarfs. These are made, with considerable Skill, from the Hair of bears and wild cattle. They paint their faces with red ocher, great quantities of which are found at a distance of some days' journey from the village. They live by hunting, game being plentiful in that country, and on indian corn, of which they always have a good crop; consequently, they have never suffered from famine. They also sow beans and melons, which are Excellent, especially those that have red seeds. Their Squashes are not of the best; they dry them in the sun, to eat them during The winter and spring. Their Cabins are very large, and are Roofed and floored with mats made of Rushes. They make all Their utensils of wood, and Their Ladles out of the heads of cattle, whose Skulls they know so well how to prepare that they use these ladles with ease for eating their sagamité.

They are liberal in cases of illness, and Think that the effect of the medicines administered to them is in proportion to the presents given to the physician. Their garments consist only of skins; the women are always clad very modestly and very becomingly, while the men do not take the trouble to cover themselves. . . .

## REASONS FOR NOT GOING FARTHER

. . . . Monsieur Jolliet and I held another Council, to deliberate upon what we should do – whether we should push on, or remain content with the discovery which we had made. After attentively considering that we were not far from the gulf of Mexico, the basin of which is at a latitude of 31 degrees 60 minutes, while we were at 33 degrees 40 minutes, we judged that we could not be more than 2 or 3 days' journey from it; and that, beyond a doubt, the Missisipi river discharges into the florida or Mexican gulf, and not to The east in Virginia, whose sea-coast is at 34 degrees latitude, – which we had passed, without, however, having yet reached the sea, – or to the west in California, because in that case our route would have been to The west, or the west-southwest, whereas we had always continued It toward the south. We further considered that we exposed ourselves to the risk of losing the results of this voyage, of which we could give no information if we proceeded to fling ourselves into the hands of the Spaniards who, without doubt, would at least have detained us as captives. Moreover, we saw very plainly that we were not in a condition to resist Savages allied to The Europeans, who were numerous, and expert in firing guns, and who continually infested the lower part of the river. Finally, we had obtained all the information that could be desired in regard to this discovery. All these reasons induced us to decide upon Returning; this we announced to the savages, and, after a day's rest, made our preparations for it.

## RETURN OF THE FATHER AND OF
## THE FRENCH. BAPTISM OF
## A DYING CHILD

After a month's Navigation, while descending Missisipi from the 42nd to the 34th degree, and beyond, and after preaching the Gospel as well as I could to the Nations that I met, we start on the 17th of July . . . to retrace our steps. We therefore reascend the Missisipi which gives us much trouble in breasting its Currents. It is true that we leave it, at about the 38th degree, to enter another river, which greatly shortens our road, and takes us with but little effort to the lake of the Ilinois [Lake Michigan].

We have seen nothing like this river that we enter, as regards its fertility of soil, its prairies and woods; its cattle, elk, deer, wildcats, bustards, swans, ducks, parroquets, and even beaver. There are many small lakes and rivers. That on which we sailed is wide, deep, and still, for 65 leagues. In the Spring and during part of The Summer there is only one portage of half a league. We found on it a village of Ilinois called Kaskasia, consisting of 74 Cabins. They received us very well, and obliged me to promise that I would return to instruct them. One of the chiefs of this nation, with his young men, escorted us to the Lake of the Ilinois, whence at last, at The end of September, we reached the bay des puantz [Green Bay], from which we had started in the beginning of June.

Had this voyage resulted in the salvation of even one soul, I would consider all my troubles well rewarded, and I have reason to presume that such is the case. For, when I was returning, we passed through the Ilinois of Peouarea, and during three days I preached the faith in all their Cabins; after which, while we were embarking, a dying child was brought to me at The water's edge, and I baptized it shortly before it died, through an admirable act of providence for the salvation of that Innocent soul.

# V

## A LETTER, ADDRESSED TO REVEREND FATHER JEAN DE LAMBERVILLE, REGARDING THE ILLINOIS MISSIONS

*(This letter, not signed, was probably written by Father Jacques Gravier, who was a member of the Illinois mission from 1688 to 1705. Lamberville was procurator for the Canadian missions.)*

****

MY REVEREND FATHER:

I send to Your Reverence The invoice of this year, 1702, for The Ilinois missions, and for The 3 fathers who are there now. I beg you not to be surprised if it be somewhat large. It is to supply clothes and provisions for three fathers, besides Brother guibort and perhaps Brother gillet, who are in need of everything; and to begin at last to supply, once for all, The principal items of all that is required for 3 missions – which have always been borrowing; which have always lacked most of the necessary articles; And wherein The missionaries have done nothing but languish. Father bineteau died there from exhaustion; but, If he had had a few drops of spanish wine, for which he asked us during his last illness, and some little dainties, – such as sugar, or other things, – or had we been able to procure some Fresh food for him, he would perhaps be still alive. Father pinet and father marest are wearing out their strength; and they are 2 saints, who take pleasure in being deprived of everything – in order, they say, that they may soon be nearer paradise. But they do not fail to tell me and to write me that I must bring some little comforts for the sick, and that these languish because they are in need of everything; and they tell the truth. For my part I am in good health, but I have no cassock, etc.; I am in a sorry plight, and the others are hardly less so.

Three winter cassocks.

3 pairs of winter hose.

3 lined cloaks.

3 summer cassocks; 3 pairs of winter and 3 of summer breeches.

3 pairs of summer hose.

3 pairs of cloth breeches for winter.

6 pairs of breeches of black duck or strong linen.

12 hempen shirts, lined; calico handkerchiefs; Cap linings.

4 hats; 3 hoods; 3 pairs of mittens.

One Livre of black Wool.

Half a livre of black and other silk.

One Livre of fine white thread.

2 livres of black thread. 1 livre of twine for Nets. 3 Lines; 3 whip – [lashes?]

3 livres of coarse white thread.

6 pairs of Shoes.

3 pairs of double-soled slippers.

3 pieces of white thread galloon.

One thousand pins.

One Ream of good and strong paper, of large size.

One Ream of small-sized paper. 3 good razors, with a whetstone.

3 sticks of spanish wax. 3 half-double caps.

12 [small] towels and 6 [small] napkins.

3 covered bowls for The sick.

12 pewter spoons, with knives and forks.

[*illegible* – 6 case-knives?] in 6 sheaths.

3 deep pewter basins with a narrow edge.

6 plates.

3 tinned kettles with lids, and strong, to hold 6 pots [about 18 pints] each.

One Syringe; one livre of Theriac; ointment, plasters, alum, vitriol, aniseed, medicines, and pastils.

One host-Iron, and shape fur cutting the wafers.

50 livres of flour, in a Barrel. 3 Tin boxes.
 One minot [1.11 bushels] of Salt, in a Barrel.
 A jar of oil.
 A Barrel of 15 pots of vinegar.
30 livres of Sugar.
 Rice, raisins, prunes.
25 pots of spanish wine, In 2 kegs.
25 pots of brandy.
 9 livres of pepper.
 One Livre of nutmegs and cloves.
 Six pairs of half-worsted hose. [Material for making]
  awnings as a protection against the gnats that infest the
  mississipi.
 One piece of strong sail cloth.
 One livre or 2 of cotton candle-wicking.
 Indian ink and cotton [*illegible*].
 A thousand nails, large, medium-sized, and small.
150 livres of powder.
 50 livres of assorted shot, large and small.
 50 livres of Bullets; [500 gun-flints].
 Ten livres of vermillion.
 Ten livres of large glass Beads – black, white and Striped.
 Ten livres of small glass Beads – white, green, and trans-
  parent.
 One gross of large Clasp-knives, with horn handles.
 One gross of round buckles, both large and medium-sized.
 One gross of small metal plates [for mirrors].
 Six gross of small belts.
 Six gross of finger-Rings.
 3 gross of awls.
 One thousand needles.
 Six boxes of gun-flints.
 Twenty gun-screws.
 One dozen [wooden?] combs.
 3 dozen Spools of fine iron wire, or Else a roll of fine wire.
 Six Bars of soap.
 Three dozen hatchets, medium-sized, large, and small.
 Three dozen medium-sized hoes.
 Three hatchets [*illegible*], 3 mattocks.
 One dozen trade shirts – large, medium-sized, and small.

Six blue capotes – large, medium-sized, and small.
Six ells of stuff for capotes, to make Breech-clouts.
Thirty livres of good tobacco.
Three dozen wax candles, and
Six livres of Wax tapers for the 3 missionaries.

The same is needed in proportion for each mission; and a chapel, with all its accessories, is required for The missionary to the Scious, since a father will be sent there; and he has need of a man. . . . You will find this a very long list, but Nothing can be Omitted from it if you wish the missionaries to have any comfort. Since it costs nothing for The fort to the Missionaries of quebec – who have Received through Monsieur d'Iberville[28] 10 times more than they asked – we Shall not be in a worse condition; and he has written to me that we should bring out engagés [indentured servants] from France, whom we could get There cheaper than here, and whose passage would cost us nothing.

# VI

✳✳✳✳✳✳✳✳✳✳✳✳✳✳✳

## LETTER BY REVEREND FATHER ÉTIENNE DE CARHEIL[29] TO MONSIEUR LOUIS HECTOR DE CALLIERES, GOVERNOR

*At Michilimakina,
the 30th of August, 1702.*

✳✳✳✳

MONSEIGNEUR:

. . . If his majesty desire to save our missions and to support the Establishment of Religion, as we have no Doubt he does, we beg him most humbly to Believe What is most true, namely; that there is no other means of doing so than to abolish completely the two Infamous sorts of Commerce which have brought the missions to the brink of destruction, and which will not long delay in destroying these if they be not abolished as soon as possible by his orders, and be prevented from ever being restored. The first is the Commerce in brandy; the second is the Commerce of the savage women with the french. Both are carried on in an equally public manner, without our being able to remedy the evil, because we are not supported by the Commandants. They – far from attempting, when we undertake to remonstrate with them, to check these trades – themselves carry them on with greater freedom than do their Subordinates and so sanction them by their example. So much is this the case that all the villages of our savages are now only Taverns, as regards drunkenness; and sodoms, as regards immorality – from which we must withdraw, and which we must abandon to the just Anger and vengeance of God.

You see by this that, in whatever manner the french trade is Established among our savages, if it be desired to still retain us among them, we must be delivered from the Commandants and from their garrisons. These, far from being necessary, are on the contrary, so pernicious that we can truly say that they are the greatest scourge of our missions. All the pretended service which it is sought to make people believe that they render to the King is reduced to 4 chief occupations, of which we beg you to Inform His majesty.

The first consists in keeping a public Tavern for the sale of brandy, wherein they trade it Continually to the savages, who do not cease to become intoxicated, notwithstanding our efforts to prevent it. The second occupation of the soldiers consists in being sent from one post to another by the Commandants in order to carry their wares and their brandy thither, after having made arrangements together; and none of them have any other object than That of assisting one another in their Traffic.

Their third occupation consists in making of their fort a place that I am ashamed to call by its proper name, where the women have found out that their bodies might serve in lieu of merchandise and would be still better received than Beaver-skins; accordingly, that is now the most usual and most Con-tinual Commerce, and that which is most extensively carried on. Whatever efforts the missionaries may make to denounce and abolish it, this traffic increases, instead of diminishing, and grows daily more and more. . . .

The 4th occupation of the soldiers is gambling, which at the times when the traders assemble sometimes proceeds to such excess that they are not satisfied with passing the whole day, but they also spend the whole night in this pursuit. But what makes their misconduct on This score still worse is, that so persistent an attachment to the game is hardly ever unaccompanied by the general Intoxication of all the players; and drunkenness is nearly always followed by quarrels that arise among them.

If occupations of this kind can be called the king's service, I admit that they have always rendered him one of Those four services. But I have observed none other than those four; and consequently, if such services be not considered necessary to the King, there has never been hitherto any necessity for keeping them here: and after they are recalled, there is no necessity of sending them back. For in reality the Commandants come here solely for the purpose of trading in concert with their soldiers, without troubling themselves about anything else. They have no intercourse with the missionaries, except with regard to Matters wherein they consider the latter useful for the furtherance of their own temporal affairs; and beyond that they are hostile to the fathers as soon as these undertake to oppose the misconduct, which being in accord neither with the service of God nor the service of the King, is nevertheless advantageous to the trade of the Commandants. . . .

It is the Commandants, it is the Garrisons, who, uniting with the brandy traders have completely desolated the missions by almost universal drunkenness and Lewdness; the civil authorities not only tolerate but permit these, inasmuch as, while able to Prevent them, they do not.

In whatever light we may consider the Commerce carried on, as regards either the Common interest of Canada, or the advancement of Christianity, It would be Infinitely more advantageous for both if the savages themselves went down annually for that purpose to Montreal, than it would be to send the french here to trade, in the way they come every Year. You ask, what would be best; to restore the 25 Permits without any posts, or to Establish posts without the 25 Permits.[30] I frankly admit that I am very much embarrassed to answer because I know not very well to what kind of posts you are pleased to refer. Are they posts solely of traders, without garrisons and without commandants; or posts that would be occupied at the same time by persons employed in Trading, and by Commandants with their garrisons, who would watch over their *safety*? . . .

Now suppose that, for the Reasons given Above, neither the garrisons with their Commandants nor the 25 Permits are Reestablished in our missions; and that the Trade of the savages cannot be Reestablished or permanently fixed with certainty at montreal. There would remain, then, no other measure for the Company to adopt than to send and maintain in our missions up here Selected persons, sober and virtuous, Intelligent, and well versed in everything connected with That trade, – and finally, such as would be fully disposed to live on terms of mutual Agreement with all the missionaries. These men should be sent, in whatever number the Company might Deem necessary and sufficient for carrying on its Trade, for attaching thereto the Savages, and for retaining them in it both by their presence and that of their wares; and by the sight, the transportation, and the Continual Sale of these wares among them. The French should be stationed in a good fort, always well provisioned, and well supplied with arms for its defense, – where Those who would have charge of the Trade would on Such occasions occupy the position of Commandants, while the others would take the place of the garrisons.

Such, monseigneur, is What we Consider the best that can be done for our missions, and the best that can be done in the Interest of the Company – which, by That means, would be sure to obtain exclusive possession of all the Beaver-skins. For there would no longer be either Commandants or garrisons – who, in spite of all the precautions that may be taken, nevertheless succeed in obtaining a considerable portion of the peltries, by an Infinite number of hidden ways, and by secret intelligence with the savages. . . .

Monseigneur,

your very humble and very obedient servant,

signed, ÉTIENNE DE CARHEIL,

of the Society of Jesus.

# VII

## SETTLEMENTS AND MISSIONS OF
## THE SOCIETY IN
## NEW FRANCE

### (1703)

*(From an account of the Canadian
missions, 1611-1710, written
by the Jesuit historian,
Joseph Jouvency.)*

✳✳✳✳

And that the Lord is with his servants and soldiers, the outcome
has proved. For, in the beginning of this year, 1703, while we
are writing these things, there are numbered in this formerly
*solitary and unexplored country* more than thirty very pros-
perous and well-equipped Missions of our Society, besides the
college of Quebec. The first of these, in sight of Quebec, at the
tenth mile-stone from the city, is called Lorette. Another is
situated in the district of Tadoussac, on the shore of the river
St. Lawrence, sixty leagues below Quebec toward the east.
Three others, above Quebec itself, extend far into the North
about Lake St. John; one in that place which takes its name
from the seven islands; another in the district of Chigutimini,
the third on the Saguenay River. There they minister to the
Montagnais . . . and other wandering tribes.

Now, if you journey toward the regions of the setting sun,
and the source of the St. Lawrence River, you will find upon its
northern bank a district called Three rivers, because there three
rivers flow together; it is distant from Quebec, seven or eight
days' journey. Here, there formerly flourished the most successful mission of the Algonquins; but it has been much weakened

through drunkenness induced by brandy, brought in by the European merchants who thus wickedly derive an easy profit. But these losses are compensated by the virtue and piety of the Abenakis. Among them a mission of three stations has been established; one located among them, not far from Quebec, on the forty-sixth parallel of latitude, distinguished by the name and patronage of St. Francis de Sales: the other two are more remote, at a place named Nipisikouit. Across the St. Lawrence River, to the South, extend the five nations of the Iroquois. There are among them seven stations of the Evangelists, scattered through a hundred and fifty leagues. Of these, six were destroyed in the war, which arose between the French and the Iroquois, about the year 1682. Peace, together with the recall of the missionaries, in the year 1702, restored all things to their previous condition. Among these Missions of the Iroquois, that one is especially flourishing which is named for St. Francis Xavier, at Montreal.

Above the Iroquois, toward the west and North, between the fortieth and the forty-fifth parallels, one may see two great lakes joined by a narrow strait; the larger one is called the lake of the Ilinois, the other the lake of the Hurons. These are separated by a large peninsula, at the point of which is situated the Mission of St. Ignatius, or Missilimakinac. Above those two lakes there is a third, greater than either, called lake superior. At the entrance of this lake has been established the Mission of Ste. Marie at the Sault. The space between this and two smaller lakes is occupied by the Outaouki [Ottawas], among whom the Society has many stations. Three such citadels of religion (for thus it is proper to call the Missions), whence she leads forth her soldiers and unfurls her sacred standards, have been located about the lake of the Ilinois; the first, among the Puteatamis [Pottawattomies], and called the Mission of St. Joseph; another, among the Kikarous, Maskoutens, and Outagamies [Foxes], and possessing the name of St. Francis Xavier, the third, among the Oumiamis, has the name of the Guardian Angel.

Below the lakes which have been mentioned, above Florida, the Ilinois roam throughout the most extensive territories. There, a very large station, named from the immaculate conception of the Virgin Mother, is divided into three Missions, and extends as far as the river Mississippi. Upon the banks of the same river is situated the mission of Baiogula [Natchez], at the thirty-first parallel of latitude; and it extends down that stream toward the gulf of Mexico.

There remains unknown to Europeans, up to the present time, an immense portion of Canada, beyond the Mississippi River, situated beneath a milder sky, well-inhabited, and abounding in animal and vegetable life. So it is, likewise, with another region far dissimilar to that, around the frozen Hudson bay, from the fifty-fifth parallel to the sixtieth or seventieth; lying at the north, plunged in snows and frosts, it even more justly implores aid, as it is afflicted by more weighty ills. Here the Society, a few years ago, first began to plant its footsteps. Not without great exertion are the gates of Tartarus, which hold burdened souls in unmerited bondage, broken down; nor did the Canadian Mission itself, now flourishing with so many settlements, all at once attain its full development. . . .

# PART FIVE

❋❋❋❋

## THE JESUITS AT
## QUEBEC

❋❋❋❋❋❋❋❋❋❋❋❋❋❋

# I

❋❋❋❋❋❋❋❋❋❋❋❋❋❋

### RELATION OF WHAT OCCURRED IN
### NEW FRANCE IN THE YEAR
### 1635

*By Father Paul le Jeune*

## OF THE CONDITION AND EMPLOYMENT
## OF OUR SOCIETY IN
## NEW FRANCE

❋❋❋❋

We have six residences in New France. The first, beginning with the first land encountered in coming into these countries, is called the Residence of Sainte Anne; it is at Cape Breton. The second is the Residence of Saint Charles, at Miscou. The third, which we are going to occupy this Autumn, the Residence of Nostredame de Recouvrance, at Kebec, near the Fort. The fourth, the Residence of Nostredame des Anges, half a league from Kebec. The fifth, the Residence of the Conception, at the three Rivers. The sixth, the Residence of Saint Joseph, at Ihonatiria, among the Hurons. I hope that we shall soon have a seventh, in the same country, but in a Village other than Ihonatiria. Now, as the vessels which go to Cape Breton and to Miscou do not go up as far as Kebec, it thus happens that we have no communication with our Fathers who are in the Residences of Sainte Anne and of Saint Charles, except by way of France; hence neither letters nor other things should be sent to us to hold for them, but they should be given to those Vessels which go to these French settlements. It follows also that I can say nothing of the things which take place in these Residences, on account of their remoteness and the little commerce we have with them.

All these Residences are maintained by the Gentlemen of the Company of New France, who have had Fortresses and dwellings for our French people built in different parts of the country, – except the Residence of Nostredame des Anges. This Residence has three great plans for the glory of our Lord; the first, to erect a College for the education of the children of the families, which are every day becoming more numerous. The second, to establish a Seminary for the little Savages, to rear them in the Christian faith. The third, to give powerful aid to the Mission of our Fathers among the Hurons and other stationary tribes. As to the College, although it is not yet built, we shall begin this year to teach a few children. Everything has its beginning; the most learned once knew only the first elements of the Alphabet.

In regard to the Seminary, we are now having one built. For a while it will be in the Residence of Nostredame des Anges; but if some pious person be found who wishes to endow it, and to support the poor little barbarians, it will have to be moved farther up the river, to a place where the Savages will not object to bring their children. I send a little boy to Your Reverence, and, if you please, you will return him to us in a couple of years; he will help to retain and teach his little compatriots; the one I did send you, and who has been returned to us, pleases us greatly. The Savages are beginning to open their eyes, and to recognize that children who are with us are well taught. . . .

### HOW IT IS A BENEFIT TO BOTH
### OLD AND NEW FRANCE, TO
### SEND COLONIES HERE

Geographers, Historians, and experience show us that every year a great many people leave France who go to enroll themselves elsewhere. For, although the Soil of our country is very fertile, the French women have this blessing, that they are still more so; and thence it happens that our ancient Gauls, in want of land, went to seek it in different parts of Europe. At present, our French people are no less numerous than our old Gauls; but they do not go forth in bands, but separately. Would it not be better to empty Old France into New, by means of Colonies, than to people Foreign countries?

Add to this, if you please, that there is a multitude of workmen in France, who, for lack of employment or of owning a little land, pass their lives in wretched want. Many of them beg their bread from door to door; some of them resort to stealing; others to larceny and secret frauds, each one trying to obtain for himself what many cannot possess. Now, as New France is so immense, so many inhabitants can be sent here that those who remain in the Mother Country will have enough honest work left them to do, without launching into those vices which ruin Republics; this does not mean that ruined people, or those of evil lives, should be sent here, for that would be to build Babylons.

Now there is no doubt that there can be found here employment for all sorts of artisans. Why cannot the great forests of New France largely furnish the Ships for the Old? Who doubts that there are here mines of iron, copper, and other metals? Some have been already discovered, which will soon be worked; and hence all those who work in wood and iron will find employment here. I do not pretend to recite all the advantages of the country; I will content myself by saying that it would be an honor and a great benefit to both old and new France to send over Emigrants and establish strong colonies in these lands, which have lain fallow since the birth of the world.

# II

✻✻✻✻✻✻✻✻✻✻✻✻✻✻✻

RELATION OF WHAT OCCURRED IN
NEW FRANCE IN THE YEAR
1639

*By Father Paul le Jeune*

OF THE JOY FELT IN NEW FRANCE AT THE
BIRTH OF MONSEIGNEUR THE DAUPHIN
AND OF A COUNCIL HELD BY
THE SAVAGES

✻✻✻✻

The most extraordinary delay in the arrival of the fleet this year had made us very uneasy, when a ship, appearing forty leagues below Kebec, sent a short letter to Monseigneur our Governor. Every one hastened to learn the news; but, as the paper contained not a word about the birth of Monseigneur the Dauphin, it checked the course of our joy. We had heard the year before that the Queen was *enceinte* and we hoped for a child whose birth would be at once a blessing and a miracle; we all thought that God's gifts would be perfected, and that we would have a Prince. This ship, which should have brought us the first news, said not a word of it. It merely informed us that other vessels were coming, from which it had been separated at sea in a heavy fog. Finally, the winds becoming favorable to our wishes, we learned that Heaven had given us a Dauphin.

Hardly had this word "Dauphin" escaped the lips of the Messengers, than joy entered into our hearts and thanksgiving into our souls. The news soon spread everywhere; the *Te Deum Laudamus* was chanted, and bonfires and fireworks were prepared with every device possible in these countries. . . .

Last year, a Canadian Savage, the son of one *Iwanchou*, a Savage captain well known to the French, went to France and was very well received by his Majesty, at whose feet he laid his Crown of Porcelain beads, as a sign that he recognized that great Prince, in the name of these nations, as their true and lawful Monarch. . . .

When this young Savage returned to his own country, he came up to Kebec with a party of his Countrymen, and went to see monsieur the Chevalier de Montmagny, our Governor to whom these gifts were brought. There happened to be present, at the time, Huron, Algonquin, and Montagnais Savages, who all admired the goodness of our Prince, whom they called their King. . . .

At the same time Ioanchou, and his son who had been in France, were asked if they would not join the others. They replied that they would go and consult their people, and, if they wished to come up here, they would bring them.

Now, I was glad to speak of the great things to be seen in France in the presence of a Savage just returned from there. "Reproach me now with falsehood," I said to them; "ask your Countryman if what I told you of the greatness of our King and of the beauty of our country be not true? And do not any more call in question what I shall hereafter tell you."

This good Savage related marvels, but according to his own range of understanding. Although he had greatly admired many things, – among others, the great multitude in Paris; the great number of cookshops; the collossal Saint Christophe of Nostre Dame, which at first sight, caused him much terror; the Coaches, which he called "rolling cabins drawn by Moose," – he admitted that nothing had so interested him as the King, when he saw him on the first day of the year, walking with his guards. He attentively observed all the soldiers marching in good order; the Swiss produced a great impression on his eyes, and the sound of their drum on his head. When he went away thence, he did not speak for the remainder of the day – so the Father who accompanied him told me – doing nothing but reflect upon what he had seen.

He related all this to his people, who listened to him with avidity. The King's piety was of powerful assistance to us in doing honor to our faith; for this good Canadian admitted that the first time he saw the King was in the house of Prayer, where he prayed to JESUS as he is prayed to here. He also stated publicly that the King had asked him if he had been baptized. This has helped us and will again help us to make these poor peoples understand the esteem in which that great Prince holds the doctrine that we teach them. In fact, as soon as this Savage had seen the King, he said to the Father who conducted him; "Let us go away. I have seen all, since I have seen the King."

To conclude this chapter; our Savages, seeing that his Majesty had sent them clothes in the French fashion, determined to send a little dress, such as is worn by Savages, to Monseigneur the Dauphin. When they handed it to me, they had the wit to say: "It is not a present that we make him, for his riches are far greater than ours; but it is a metawagan – a small toy to amuse his little Son, who may perhaps take pleasure in seeing how our children are dressed."

We send this little dress to Your Reverence. However, as smallpox greatly prevails among our Savages, I do not know whether it is advisable to present it, for fear that it may carry even the slightest contagion with it. It is true that I had it in my possession before the disease broke out among those that gave it to me; but, when so sacred a personage is concerned, a danger even a thousand leagues distant is to be dreaded.

## OF THE NUNS RECENTLY ARRIVED
## IN NEW FRANCE, AND OF
## THEIR OCCUPATION

. . . . When we were informed that a bark was about to arrive at Kebec, bearing a College of Jesuits, an establishment of Hospital Nuns, and a Convent of Ursulines, the news seemed at first almost a dream; but at last, descending toward the great river, we found that it was a reality. As this holy band left the ship, they fell on their knees and kissed the soil of their beloved country – for thus they called these regions. From a floating prison were seen issuing those virgins consecrated to God, as fresh and rosy as when they had left their homes. All Ocean, with its waves and tempests, had not injured their health in the slightest degree.

Monsieur the Governor received them with all possible honor. We led them to the Chapel; the *Te Deum laudamus* was chanted; the Cannon thundered on all sides. Then we conducted them to the houses set apart for them until such time as they should have others more suitable for their duties. On the following day they were taken to the Residence of Sillery, where the Savages dwell. When they saw these poor people assembled in the Chapel, offering their prayers and singing the articles of our creed, the tears fell from their eyes. On going thence, they visited the settled families and the neighboring Cabins. Madame de la Pelterie,[31] who led the party, could not meet a little Savage girl without embracing and kissing her, with marks of affection so sweet and emphatic that these poor barbarians stood astonished and edified, — all the more that they themselves are cold in their greetings.

The newly arrived Fathers were set to work; they were called upon to baptize some Savages. Madame de la Pelterie is already the godmother of several. She could not contain herself; she wished to be everywhere, whenever the Savages were in question.

These visits being soon over, these good women retired into their seclusion. Into the Hospital went the three Nuns sent by Monseigneur the Most Reverend Archbishop of Rouen. The three Ursulines withdrew to a private house. Soon afterwards, we had six savage girls given to Madame de la Pelterie or to the Ursulines; and some French girls began going to them for instruction; so that they already perform the duties of their order. But if ever they have a house with sufficient accommodation, and the means to feed the savage children, they will perhaps have so many of these as to weary them.

As for the Hospital, the Nuns were not yet lodged, and their baggage had not yet arrived, when sick people were brought to them. We had to lend our straw beds and mattresses that they might perform the first act of charity. They had sick persons to nurse and had nothing to give them; but the charity of Monsieur our Governor is delightful. Even if it is necessary to refuse some poor afflicted Savage, one cannot do everything at the first stroke. If the Savages are capable of astonishment, they will experience it here; for among them no heed is paid to the sick, especially if they are considered sick unto death; they are looked upon as beings of another world, with whom is held no intercourse, no conversation.

# III

## OF THE RESIDENCE AT SILLERY, AND
## HOW THE SAVAGES THERE
## SPEND THE YEAR

*(From the* Relation *for 1642-43, written
by Father Barthélémy Vimont.)*

✳✳✳✳

The little village of St. Joseph, called Sillery, two scant leagues distant from Quebec, is composed of about 35 or 40 families of Christian Savages who have settled there, and live there all year, except the times for their hunting; these are often joined by many of those who are still roving, – partly to receive some assistance, partly to be instructed in the mysteries of our holy faith. This number will seem small to those who are not acquainted with the state of a roving Savage; but sufficiently large to those who are thus acquainted, and know the life which the poor wretches formerly led.

The good reputation of the Savages who have betaken themselves thither, and who there publicly exercise their Christian duties, has spread abroad on all sides; from Tadoussac and Miskou, even to the Hurons, nearly all speak of imitating them. These resident families are composed of two sorts of persons, – one Montagnais, the other Algonquins. The Montagnais are those who reside nearer Kebec, and are thus called on account of our high mountains. The Algonquins are further back, – some are of the Island and from various places, extending toward the Hurons; the others are neighbors of the Montagnais, and as if mingled with them. The knowledge of God, and intercourse with the French of Kebec, has rendered the latter more supple and docile; the others, though nearly all ruined and reduced to nothing, have remained in a strange pride, and have hitherto occasioned us great hindrances to the conversion of the other Algonquins, and of the Hurons themselves, who are obliged to pass through their country, in order to come down hither.

We have, as yet, for all these resident families only four little houses, on the French plan; to these we are going to add, this Autumn, two others, begun last Winter, by means of some alms which have been given us for this purpose. We are planning for still another, next Spring. The houses are built, half on our side, and half on the side of the Hospital, which is separated from us by a hill or mound about sixty paces wide. The Montagnais have chosen our side, the Algonquins have taken that of the Hospital; the principal Savages are lodged in these houses on the French plan; the others dwell, in their fashion, under cabins of bark, – each on the side chosen by his own tribe, waiting until we can procure for them also some small buildings, as for their companions.

The principal advantages of these houses are the little lofts in which they bestow their provisions, and their little belongings, which formerly became scattered and lost for want of a place in which to keep them. It has not been feasible to do more; for, in proportion to the houses, it is necessary to aid in clearing lands for those who are lodged. At the start, we had means of supporting eight workmen at Sillery; they are at present reduced to four; and still we hear from France that the amount of the donation of the late Monsieur de Sillery, intended for their maintenance, is detained in France. I am very certain of one thing, – that it is still more difficult to continue and maintain it than it was to begin it.

Now let us observe how the Savages have spent their years at Sillery. The ships weighed anchor from before Kebec the 7th of October of last year. Their departure produces a wonderful silence here, and directs each man's attention to his own family, in deep tranquillity.

Our Savages of Sillery, and some others who had united with them, continued their fishing for Eels which they had begun some time before; this is a very fertile harvest for the gathering at Kebec and in the surrounding regions, every year, from the beginning of September to the end of October, in the great river of St. Lawrence. At that time, they found this fish in prodigious abundance; the French salt it, the Savages smoke it, both make provision thereof for the Winter. The Savages leave their little houses to carry on this fishing, and encamp a musket range away, so that the refuse of the fish which they prepare may not infect them. Their fishing done, which was toward the beginning of November, they returned to their houses, and filled their little stores with smoked fish.

They were no sooner assembled than thirteen canoes of the nation of the Atikamegues [Whitefish Indians] came to see them, in order to winter with them, and to receive instruction. Father Buteux, who had come down from the three Rivers to winter at Sillery, had charge of the instruction of both parties, – that is to say, of the Montagnais and of the Atikamegues. They lived together, speaking the same language. Father Dequen had for his share the instruction of the Algonquins.

This is the plan we followed all the winter: Father Dequen went every morning to the hospital, in the Algonquin quarter, to say Mass: men, women, and children all were there. The Chapel and the ward of the sick were often filled. Before Mass, the Father pronounced aloud in their language the prayers, which each one also repeated aloud. After noon, I assumed charge of teaching the catechism to the Algonquin children. They assembled in the ward of the sick, with as much diligence and fervor as those of our France. If their stability were equally firm, they would yield to them in nothing. The reward for catechism was a knife, or a piece of bread, at other times a chaplet, – sometimes a cap, or an axe, for the tallest and most intelligent; it is an excellent opportunity for relieving the misery of these poor peoples. The parents were charmed with the fervor of their children, who went through the cabins to show their prizes.

The Hospital Nuns often intoned, at prayers and at catechism, some hymns in Algonquin speech. The Savages take much pleasure in singing, and succeed in it very well, too. When they were in need, the catechism was followed by a little feast, or sagamité, to relieve their hunger. The Nuns contributed, in their turn, to the necessary expenses; and, generally speaking, in addition to the care and succor of the sick, they have often had two or three of the cabins of the poorest on their hands; it is incredible what expenses one is obliged to incur on such occasions; the misery and necessity is such that conscience is compelled thereto. So much for the Algonquins.

Father Buteux has observed the same plan for the Montagnais and Atikamegues, except that when the latter had betaken themselves a little way into the woods on a small eminence near Sillery, he was obliged to go hither every day after Mass, and toward evening, when he assembled the men and the women apart. The snows were from three to four feet deep. I have repeatedly seen him return at evening – night having already set in – with a lantern in his hand, which the impetuous wind snatched from him or extinguished, and then overturned him in the snows from top to bottom of the hill. That may astonish those who have known him in France, – infirm to the last degree, and nearly always on the sick list.

In this manner the Savages spent the first part of the winter. Toward the middle of January, the snows being already deep and abundant, they all withdrew from the cabins at Sillery, and went to about a quarter of a league from Kebec, to make their sledges there, and to begin their first hunt; they remained there about three weeks. Father Buteux followed the Atikamegues, and went to lodge in their cabins. They went a quarter of a league every day, so as to come to Quebec and hear Mass, notwithstanding the rigor of the cold and the snows. Usually they went into the Chapel of the Ursulines, where Father Buteux taught them. They also went very often to the Nuns' parlor, and asked to repeat their prayers, in order to learn them better. The Ursulines showed them every sort of charity, – gave them to eat, and spared nothing of what they had to assist them. They do no less than this, throughout the year, for the Algonquins and Montagnais, when they come to Quebec. These are inevitable expenses, for those who have undertaken to aid the Savages.

They all left their cabins toward the beginning of February, and went into the great woods for the chase of the Moose. The day after their departure, as I was going from Kebec to Sillery, I found a single cabin of twelve or thirteen invalids, old men and children, whom the Savages had commended to me the evening before, and had asked me to send them to the Hospital. When they saw me pass, they took their coverings of bark, followed me as best they could, and came away to the Hospital to spend their winter, partly in the ward of the sick, partly in a cabin near the Hospital.

The Savages remained hardly two months in their great hunt; several returned for the Easter holidays. Each cabin usually contains a paper which marks the feast days. Jean Baptiste with his band returned on Wednesday in Passion Week, and was present in good time next day, for the washing of feet, which occurred at the Hospital; then we prepared for all a feast that was magnificent for this country. Five Hurons who wintered at Sillery and formed a little seminary there, marvelled at this festival, which Father de Brébeuf explained to them (they do not fail to relate these tidings in their own country).

Toward the end of April, all the Savages again rally together; each returns to his own quarter and sets up his cabin, prepares his little store, dresses his skins, and comes to instruction, where the same order is observed as in the autumn. When the earth is altogether free from snow, each one visits his field, and begins to till it. It was a pleasure to see them going to work. But this pleasure hardly lasted; for scarcely had they finished planting their Indian corn, when the rumors of incursions and ravages by the Iroquois obliged them to form a small body of warriors, and go to the fort of Richelieu and to the 3 rivers, in order to confront their enemies. But the disastrous news of the death of the King and of Monseigneur the Cardinal, and then the want of the succor of arms and soldiers which we were expecting from France, made them return to Sillery, quite sad; and, as the ships were very late, and as provisions failed them, they broke up into little bands, and went hunting toward Tadoussac, continually removing from their enemies, and awaiting the ships.

# IV

## EXTRACTS FROM THE JOURNAL
## OF THE JESUITS AT QUEBEC
## (1645-68)

### JOURNAL BEGUN,
### 1645

❊❊❊❊

*October*

On the 17th, Chrestiennaut was received into our service, at wages of thirty écus a year, and was sent to 3 rivers to serve there as Cook and Clothier, – in a word, for everything. He had come hither from france in Monsieur de repentigny's retinue; and had become discontented there, so that he had resolved to retreat to the woods rather than go back [to France]; there was no written contract with him.

On the 19th, we began to build an oven at our house, after having asked permission from Messieurs the owners of the house.

On the same day there left the house a little box, in which were 3 or 4 savage garments, all complete, to be presented to the king by Monsieur de repentigny, – because the king had expressed a desire that something from over here should be sent him. The warehouse had borne the main expense thereof.

When I arrived at montreal, they had prepared a timber dwelling for our Fathers, and it seemed that there was nothing more to be done than to raise it; but when they were on the point of doing so, the vessels arrived, bringing orders from france to those who commanded at Montreal, to employ all the workmen for other things, – namely, in erecting a hospital, for which large funds had been received in the preceding years; and yet no beginning had been made. *Monsieur de maisonneuve*, who was then at Montreal, found it hard to tell this news to our Fathers; I took it upon myself to do so, and to persuade them to regard the matter favorably; afterwards they flung the cat at my legs, as if I were the one who had hindered that work.

### November, 1645

On the 4th, we were Invited, father Vimon and I, to witness the marriage Contract of Monsieur Giffar's daughter; we were present, but we did not sign it. Monsieur the governor and several others signed.

On the 6th, Monsieur Nicolet again took away an oratory completely furnished, to the Isle aux oyes; there was a gilded silver chalice, a chasuble of white damask, etc. We gave him two cakes of candle wax, and 3 large paper Images; and we lent him two books – the life of Jesus Christ, and the abridgment of dupont.

On the 12th, we give Mademoiselle giffar some black stuff from an old cassock, for lining sleeves.

On the 21st occurred the marriage and the nuptials of Marie Giffar and the son of Monsieur de Maure, at which father Vimon was present.

On the 27th, Marriage of the daughter of Monsieur Couillar to The son of Jean Guion; there were two violins, for the 1st time.

### December, 1645

On the 3rd the Ursulines sent dinner to the house, a perfect banquet indeed. It was the 1st Sunday in Advent when Father Dendemare began to preach there, and I to the Hospital Nuns.

About this time we began to make bread at the house, – not only because that made for us at the warehouse oven was not good, but because we wished to use the corn of the land, which they did not use at the warehouse.

On the 17th, Began the Jubilee granted by Innocent X. The Ursulines, among others, gave noble alms of Cloth to the french and savage poor; as for us, our chief Alms were 7 loaves, each of the value of 15 sols, for as many persons as we were in this house at Quebek, – however that was exchanged for cloth, shoes and linen, of which things the poor people had more need.

On the 23rd of December, the Ceremonies of baptism were completed upon Caterine, wife of Atironta, and on her son mathieu, aged two years; this took place in the chapel at Quebek; they sat in Monsieur the governor's pew, at the start, and were thereby introduced to the Church. Monsieur Tronquet, secretary to monsieur the Governor, was godfather to the little one; and Madame de la ferté, the newly married daughter of monsieur Giffar, was godmother to Caterine, who received her 1st Communion at Midnight.

The 1st stroke of the midnight mass rang at eleven o'clock, the 2nd, a little before the half-hour; and then they began to sing two airs – *Venez, mon Dieu*, etc., and *Chantons noe*, etc. Monsieur de la ferté sang the bass; St. martin Played the violin; there was also a german flute, which proved to be out of tune when they came to the Church. We had finished a little before midnight; they nevertheless sang the *Te Deum*, and a little later a cannon shot was fired as the Signal of midnight, when mass began.

There were four candles in the Church in small iron candlesticks in the form of a Bracket, and that is enough. There were, besides, two great kettles full of fire, furnished by the warehouse in order to warm the chapel; they were kindled beforehand, on the bridge. Directions had been given to remove them after mass, but that having been neglected, the fire caught in the night on the floor under one of the kettles, in which there were not enough ashes at the bottom. But fortunately, *dirigente Domino*, the fire did not appear till toward 5 o'clock in the morning, above our hall or refectory, and kitchen, in which was pierre gontier, our Cook – who, perceiving this, immediately went up and, without other noise, put out the fire.

There were at Sillery, this year, about 167 souls, all Christians or Catechumens – 98 Communicants, 47 not qualified for Confession, 14 qualified for Confession alone, the rest were considered Catechumens.

### January, 1646

They Saluted Monsieur the Governor, – to wit, the soldiery with their arquebuses; *Item*, the Habitans in a body. He forestalled us, and was here at 7 o'clock to greet all our fathers. I went to greet him after high mass; (another time we must anticipate him). Monsieur giffar also came to see us, and the nuns sent letters early in the morning, to offer their Compliments. The Ursulines also sent many beautiful New-year's gifts, with tapers, rosaries, etc.; and, toward the dinner, two handsome pieces of pastry. I sent them two Images of St. Ignace and St. françois Xavier in enamel. We gave Monsieur Giffar a book of father bonnet's about the life of our Lord; to Monsieur de Chastelets one of the little volumes of Drexellius *de Aeternite*; to Monsieur bourdon a galilean telescope in which there was a compass; and to others, reliquaries, Roasaries etc. We gave a Crucifix to the woman who washes the Church linen, 4 handkerchiefs to the wife of Abraham, and to him a bottle of brandy; two handkerchiefs to robert hache and then two more that he asked for. The Ursulines sent to beg that I would go to see them before the end of the day. I went thither and also greeted Madame de la pelleterie, who sent New-year's gifts; I came near omitting that, and it is not proper to omit it.

On the 3rd or 4th of January, Monsieur the Governor sent 3 capons and 6 pigeons.

At evening on the 5th, Monsieur Giffar gave a bottle of hippocras; the hospital mothers a cake and 6 wax Candles; and the next day they sent a fine dinner.

From the 15th to the 21st the savages departed to go to the chase; there remained at Sillery about 22 savages, whom the hospital and our Fathers undertook to assist.

On the Sunday before Septuagesima, Madame Marsolet, having to prepare bread for consecration, desired to present it with the greatest possible display; she had it furnished with a toilet, – a crown of gauze or linen puffs around it. She wished to add candles, and quarter-écus at the Tapers, but seeing that we were not willing to allow her this, she nevertheless had it carried with the toilet and the Crown of puffs. However, before consecrating it, I had all that removed, and blessed it with the same simplicity that I had observed with all the preceding portions, especially with that of Monsieur the Governor, – fearing lest this change might occasion Jealousy and Vanity.

### February, 1646

On the 12th, while returning from the benediction at the hospital, I met two Hurons coming from three rivers, who reported the news *of the death of father Anne de noüe*. He started from 3 rivers to go to richelieu, to spiritually assist the garrison, on the 30th of January, in company with two soldiers and a Huron. They lay down for the night, 6 leagues above 3 rivers; but the Father left them after midnight, in order to send people to meet them and relieve them of their sledge; and he set forth *by the light of the moon*. But the sky became overcast, and it began to snow. His companions follow him by the trail of his snowshoes, and at last they find him, 4 leagues above richelieu, – kneeling in a hollow of the snow, with his arms crossed and his eyes raised to Heaven, his hat and snowshoes near him.

### *April, 1646*

The 1st Day was easter, which was very beautiful.

The Ursuline mothers of the Incarnation employed nearly the whole of Lent in painting two pieces of Architecture to match the Tabernacle of the parish church; Monsieur bourdon painted some steps.

The savages returned from the chase toward the middle of April and came back quite rich and burdened.

On the 26th I held a Consultation with reference to father Jogues's journey to the Annieronons.

On the 17th or 18th of April, the river was free, and planting began a little before that.

The savages vigorously began everywhere to till the soil. At Sillery they freshly prepared more than 15 arpents [12.6 acres] of land; at 3 rivers, more than 30 savage families began cultivation; *Item*, at Montreal. The french on their side did no less.

### *July, 1646*

On the 4th, two Abnaquiois Captains came to Monsieur the governor, to beg him to make arrangements for a black gown to go to the Abnaquiois, to Instruct them. Monsieur the governor sent them back to me, and I put them off till Autumn, in order to take time to consider the matter. They were given a bag of Indian corn for a Parting Gift, some tobacco, some fish, etc.; and we gave them a feast, and also one to the principal persons of Sillery.

On the 8th, a little savage girl named Charité, aged 5½, died at the Ursulines'; she was interred at the french Cemetary, where her Father was buried. She was borne thither by 4 domestics of the Ursulines, with 4 others bearing torches, and 2 french girls and two savage girls holding the corners of the pall.

The savages of Sillery kill a cow of monsieur Nicolas, which had been in their corn; she was valued at 75 livres. The savages were summoned by Monsieur the governor, to do Justice in this matter, and he ordered them that they should pay 6 Beavers, which was done, – with the assurance that when they should complain, Justice would be done for them for the damage which the cows might have wrought in their corn.

### September, 1646

It was the 20th, when Monsieur de maisonneuve arrived; and on the 23rd arrived Monsieur de repentigny.

With Monsieur de repentigny were *father Quentin* and some men both for the Hurons and for work down here; *Item,* a Young gentleman from the house of Courtené, who had been converted at la rochelle and had subsequently made a vow to go to the Hurons. But it proved that he was *only a swindler,* who had appeared in England as grandson to the house of Sancerre, and nephew to Monsieur desnoyers, – who made a pretense of intending to become a heretic. But learning that news from france was on the way, in consequence of information that had been given about him, he fled; He played a thousand tricks here, and finally avowed, or lied, that he *was a benedictine religious,* – a professed, for several years, – and that he was a subdeacon; and it was affirmed here that he *had entered, at Alençon, a monastery of benedictine nuns,* where he had heard the confession of a dying nun. He affected to wish to remain, and was enraged because they had written about him that he was a bastard; but those who had seen him in England whispered to him to be quiet; and he then went away. He cheated us by more than 200 livres, which we advanced for him.

### 1646, October

On the 28th, bastien entered our service for 100 livres in wages and a pair of shoes.

On the last Day of October the vessels sailed; father Quentin was the only one of Ours on board. With them returned the sons of Monsieur de repentigny, Monsieur Couillar and monsieur giffar, and the nephews of Monsieur deschastelets, – all *rogues,* for the most part, who had played a thousand tricks on the other voyage; and they all were given high salaries.[32]

They are making a new oven and a brewery at Sillery.

We begin with 6 men to quarry stone and to prepare the site for the clergy-house and the Church.

They caught, this year, forty thousand eels, most of which were sold at half an écu the hundred. They began to fish for them in August, and they finished about the 9th or 10th of November.

In october, father le Jeune exhibited a picture to the Savages at Sillery, which had come from the queen, – containing her portrait, that of the king, etc. At the same time they were given three Blankets and three arquebuses, at the expense of the warehouse; and we made a feast for them.

### 1646, November

On the 14th, Madame de la pelleterie sent a present here. It was a package, in which there was an Alter-stone and a small missal; two cloths, of which one was Damask; two dozen napkins, and two sheets, – which were given to our brother liegeois.

A few days later, Sister Charlotte sent four brasses, and more, of blue cloth, and a brasse and a half of red cloth; and several thousand porcelain beads, – all for the savages, as something which had been given her for this purpose.

On the last Day of the year, they gave a performance at the warehouse, Enacting the *sit*.[33] Our Fathers were present, – in deference to Monsieur the governor, who took pleasure therein, as also did the savages, – that is, fathers de Quen, Lalemant, and defretat: all went well, and there was nothing which could not edify. I begged Monsieur the governor to excuse me from attendance.

### The Year 1647,
### January

On the 1st, I went at the 2nd bell for mass to salute Monsieur the governor.

The Hospital nuns sent a letter by Monsieur de St. Sauveur, and two boxes of Lemon-peel by a man.

The Ursulines sent a letter, a keg of prunes, a Rosary and a paper Image.

There were sent us, by Monsieur the governor, 4 Capons, two bustards, and 8 young pigeons; by others, some 10 or 12 pieces of other poultry.

On the 2nd, we gave a dinner to Monsieur de *St. Sauveur, Monsieur the prior, and Monsieur Nicolet.*

We sent to Sillery a bustard and four capons.

To the Ursulines, a picture of St. Joseph;

7 or 8 pairs of Savage shoes to our servants.

I went on the 4th of the month to Sillery. On the morning of the 5th occurred the renewal of the vows of father gabriel *lalemant and of father defretat.* I made a feast for the Savages and gave them 6 loaves.

On the 7th, the Hospital nuns regaled us magnificently.

On the 27th of february, there was a ballet at the warehouse; it was the wednesday in shrovetide. Not one of our fathers or brethren was present; also none of the sisters of the hospital and the Ursulines.

About this time one of our cows with calf was drowned in the St. Charles river; she broke through the ice.

Toward the end of the month, Noel, Jean baptiste, and other savages of Sillery returned from the chase; the fear of the yroquois caused them to hasten.

This month, all the Timber for our house was brought over the snow by our oxen.

### May, 1647, and June

On the 10th the 1st fish were taken, and among others a salmon.

On the 22nd, Monsieur the governor departed, and I with him, for 3 rivers.

On the 4th of June, we set out to return from 3 rivers; on the 5th we arrived at Quebek. The same Day, a Shallop arrived from 3 rivers, which informed us that the son of Ignace otouolti had returned from the yroquois, – who announced the death, or rather the murder, of father Jogues and his companion Lalande, for whom the next day we said a high mass for the dead. . . .

On the 20th of June, the 1st vessel arrived at Tadousak. That same vessel brought the 1st Horse, of which the habitans made a present to Monsieur the governor.

*January, 1649*

On the 19th occurred the first execution by the hand of the hangman, in the case of a Creature of 15 or 16 years, a thief. At the same time they accused Monsieur Abraham of having violated her: he was imprisoned for this, and his trial was postponed till the arrival of the vessels. On the 19th of february, The 2nd execution of Justice took place.

The winter's Work was to pile sand for building, and wood for heating.

*May, 1649*

Return of the Shallops from 3 rivers and Montreal, where famine was found on all sides. We succored the people down here, in the matter of seed and food with 16 casks of wheat sent from 3 rivers, and several puncheons of peas and Indian corn; and furthermore by the grist of the mill, – making in all more than 40 casks of grain.

*July, 1649*

On the 10th and 17th, the Abnakiois arrived, to the number of 30. They brought letters from the English. There was one from Mademoyselle de repentigny to her husband, dated 31st of July, 1648, with news of the death of Monsieur de chastelets.

On the 20th at night, arrived the sad news of the destruction of the Hurons, *and of the martyrdom of 3 fathers. . . .*

*March, 1652*

On the second day of March, 12 Hurons, six Algonquins and ten Algonquin women, having left Three Rivers for Montreal, were attacked on the way by the Iroquois. *Desiderati sunt decem Hurones,* – Torotati, burned; Athohonchiwanne, killed; Ora'kwi, Otarawia, burned.

On the 4th of April, Father Buteux left Three Rivers for his Mission to the Atikamegues, with Tsondoutannen, a Huron, and fontarabie.

*May, 1652*

On the 10th day of May, Father Jacques Buteux, in company with a frenchman named fontarabie and a Huron named Thomas Tsondoutannen, was killed by a band of 14 Iroquois.

The two frenchmen remained dead on the spot; the Huron was Led away captive. This took place on the Three Rivers, at the third portage. The Huron afterward escaped, and arrived at Three Rivers on the 28th, giving news of the disaster.

On the 13th of the same month of May, the Algonquins, having gone up for trade to the whitefish tribe, fell into the ambushes of that band of 14 who had killed Father Bureux.

15th. Two Huron women, mother and daughter, Annendok and Atondech, with a little son four years old, were seized at Montreal by a band of 50 or 60 Iroquois. They had gone to a secluded place, to get some meat from a Moose, which four frenchmen had killed there.

On the 26th, a troop of 50 Iroquois killed the cowherd at Montreal, named Antonie Róos, near the hill St. Louys.

### August, 1652

On the 10th, news arrived from Montreal that, on the 29th of July, two Iroquois, having slipped in under cover of the corn, had attacked Martine, wife of Antoine Primot, – who, by defending herself courageously, gave the soldiers of the fort time to come to her aid, and put the enemy to flight. She received six shots, not one of which was mortal.

On the 18th, 4 frenchmen were attacked by 8 Iroquois canoes, between 3 Rivers and the Cape; Maturin Guillet and Le Boujonnier were killed on the spot. Plassez, a surgeon, and Rochereau, were taken away as captives.

19th. 2 french shallops having been in search of the cattle of 3 Rivers, – killed or scattered by the Iroquois, above 3 Rivers, along the lake, – the following persons were killed or carried away captive:

> Monsieur Du Plessis, the Governor.
> Monsieur Grandmesnil.
> Guillaume Isabelle.
> francheville, captive.
> Poisson.
> Turcot.
> Normanville, captive.
> Du Puis.
> Matris Belhomme, burned.

SOLDIERS

Langoulmois, killed.
La Palme, captive.
La Gravé.
St. Germain.
Chaillon.
Des Lauriers, died from his wounds.

### May, 1665

On the 5th, Monsieur de Mesy, the Governor, died.

On the 14th, father Alloues left for his mission among the Outawats, accompanied by two of our Servants, La tour and Nicolas.

### June, 1665

Father Thiery beschefer arrived on the 19th, in Le Gangneur's Ship, with 4 Companies of the Carignan regiment.

And on the 30th, father Claude bardy and Father francois duperon arrived, with Monseigneur de Tracy and 4 other Companies.

### July, 1665

On the 16th, Captain poulet arrived, with Monsieur bourdon, 12 Horses, 8 girls, and others.

On the 23rd, the first 4 Companies left to commence fort richelieu; father Chaumonot went with them.

### September, 1665

The 12th. The *st. sebastien* arrived, having on board Monsieur de Courcelles, the governor, and Monsieur Talon, the Intendant.

The 14th. The Ship called la Justice arrived, with more than 100 sick in all. Most of them were placed in the hospital, some in the sick-ward, and some in the Church. Many of them died.

### October, 1665

The 1st. 4 companies departed, to wait for Monseigneur de Tracy at three Rivers.

The 2nd. The ship from Normandy arrived, with 82 girls and women – among others, 50 from a charitable institution in

Paris, where they have been very well taught. *Item,* 130 laboring men, all in good health; an excellent cargo for the company, and at good prices; all the communities had on board all that comes to them from france.

### *November, 1665*

The 10th.   The earth was white with snow.

The 15th.   A vessel arrived from Richelieu, bringing us the body of Father Francois du Peron, who died on the 10th at fort st. Louys. In the evening, 5 soldiers brought the body in a coffin of boards that Monsieur sorel, the governor of Richelieu, had ordered to be made for him, after going to receive him at the water's edge with all his soldiers under arms. We also learned that he had had him guarded all the night, with lighted tapers around him. We had the body placed in the room occupied by the congregation. As he had been dead 7 days, we did not open the coffin.

The 16th.   We assembled at half past nine in the morning and issued forth in procession. Master Julien garnier bore the cross; two of our little pupils, the candlesticks; two others, the censer and the holy water. We said the office, at which *Monseigneur de Tracy* assisted. He was buried in the vault of the chapel, near the confessional on the side of the street. There remains only enough room for one more body.

# V

✱✱✱✱✱✱✱✱✱✱✱✱✱✱

## REVENUES OF THE
## JESUITS IN
## CANADA
## (1701)

✱✱✱✱

We, the undersigned, Religious of the Society of Jesus in Canada, in obedience to the order of his majesty which has been made known to us by Monsieur the Chevalier de Calliere, governor and lieutenant-general in all northern new france, and by Monsieur de Champigny, intendant of the country, do Certify that our fixed Revenues and Perquisites, with both our Taxes and obligations, are as follows:

The King, in his liberality gives us in Canada, for the maintenance of our missions among all the foreign nations of this country, in an extent of 7 to 800 leagues, a pension from the state of 5,000 livres[34]

And, besides, in a gratuity from the custom-duties ................................................................ 315 livres

*Item,* for the 3rd Instructor at the College of Quebec ............................................................ 400 livres

There is also a charitable donation, a gift made by his majesty to the Abnaquis and the iroquois converted to the faith, to assist the orphans, widows, old people, And poor, from which neither we nor the missionaries who have charge of Those savages have profited in any manner. This gift and alms amounts to ............ 1,500 livres

## THE REVENUE FROM OUR OWN
## PROPERTY AT QUEBEC

| | |
|---|---:|
| Our house in the lower town is rented at .......... | 300 livres |
| That in the upper town is rented at ................ | 120 livres |
| Our mill close by the College may, unless there be unusual expenses, yield a revenue of .... | 300 livres |
| A little piece of land opposite quebec, at Coste de lauzon ................................................. | 30 livres |
| The Estate of nostre Dame des anges, where there are mills and farms, *cens et rentes,* and tolls upon the little River St. Charles ................ | 1,205 livres |
| The Seigniory of Sillery, on account of the rents from the tenants, the eel-fisheries and a mill, about ......................................................... | 250 livres |
| The Estate of St. gabriel, the soil of which is almost everywhere sterile and unprofitable, about ................................................................. | 40 livres |
| The Seigniory of Batiscan, in seigniorial rents and for the mill, about ........................................ | 300 livres |
| Cap de la Magdelaine, which is a sandy piece of land, without trees for firewood, sterile, and abandoned by nearly all the inhabitants who had established themselves there, may yield .... | 160 livres |
| The Little piece of land at Three Rivers, about ................................................................. | 60 livres |
| La Prairie de la magdelaine, and [the parish] of St. lambert, where there is a mill and domain, and rents from some tenants who have remained and are almost all Ruined by the iroquois war ......................................................... | 385 livres |
| The Perquisates in either *lots* [*lods*] *et ventes,* or old debts, or similar matters ........................ | 280 livres |
| Our revenue in france, expenses and charges defrayed, which we receive here, may amount, at the most, to ...................................................... | 4,000 livres |
| | |
| Thus all the Revenues of the jesuit fathers of Canada may amount to ................................. | 13,145 livres |

It is True that, when the years are good, this may be increased by 1,000 livres, or thereabout; but, when they are bad, – either through the seasons, or through war, which causes everything to become dear in distant countries, – the revenues diminish accordingly, and the expenses greatly increase.

## THE EXPENDITURES

From the above Revenues we must feed, clothe, and furnish with necessaries our fathers and brethren who are here, – forty-eight Religious, and nine perpetual domestics called "donnez," almost all of whom are aged and worn out in the missions; so are also most of the fathers, who have grown old and are Broken down by the arduous labors of such missions. We have also in our missions at least fourteen men as hired servants, to take the missionaries in canoes to the remote places where the savages live, to furnish them with wood, and to help them in other like ways.

There must be added the maintenance of our sacristies, and of our churches or chapels in the missions, and the repairs of our buildings; the expenses for all the journeys of the missionaries coming and going; and, above all, the great outlays for carrying to the missionaries at 3, 4, and 500 leagues from quebec, all their necessaries, and the alms to the poor, both french and Savages. Thus we have only a very moderate amount with which to provide for so many expenses; and, besides more than 6,000 livres that we actually owe, we have to pay annually an amortisable rent of 1,000 livres.

Our principal establishments are: the College of Quebec, where there are 18 Religious; It is to this place that those whom the severe fatigues of these missions have rendered unfit for service retire.

The Residence of montreal, where there are four Religious.

The mission of the iroquois of the sault, near montreal, where there are four fathers.

That of St. Francois de salle, composed of abnaquis, loups, and sokokis, where there are 2 priests, jesuits missionaries.

The mission of the abnaquis af acadia, near the English, where there are three missionary fathers. In the missions of the outaois, islinois, miamis, scioux, and other nations, to the frontier of the mississipy region, there are eleven jesuit priests and four brethren.

At the mission of laurette, where dwell the remnant of the huron nation, one jesuit priest.

Moreover, two and sometimes three fathers from the College of Quebec leave in the spring for the missions of the Papina-chois, of tadoussac, of Chikoutimy, of the mistassins, and of lake St. John, and do not return until far into the autumn; and often some one of them even spends there the winter also. Done at Quebec, this 4th of October, 1701; and in testimony of the above, we have signed the present declaration as exact and true. Signed, therefore, martin bouvart, rector of the College of quebec, and superior of the missions of the Society of Jesus in new france; françois Vallant, and pierre Rafaix.

# VI

✳✳✳✳✳✳✳✳✳✳✳✳✳✳✳

## MEMOIR BY FATHER CLAUDE GODEFROI COQUART[35] UPON THE POSTS OF THE KING'S DOMAIN
### (1750)

### CHEKOUTIMI

✳✳✳✳

The Post of chekoutimi is 30 leagues from Tadoussac, on the upper Saguenai; two leagues higher than this post, the saguenai is no longer navigable, except for canoes. This post is the most valuable of the whole domain, on account of the quantity of Peltries which it produces – 3,000 Livres, and often more, of Beaver-skins, and about 2,000 Martens in ordinary years; last year, there were more than 3,000 of the latter, besides skins of bears, Lynxes, and otters. In a word, according to The information of the agent himself, his post has, several times during his residence there, produced more than 40,000 livres' worth of Peltries. Consequently, it pays expenses at a smaller profit than is made at the other posts. On the post of Chekoutimi depend Lake St. John, the Mistassins, and Chomoukchwan.

1st.   The savages come but little to the Post, except in the months of May, june and july. There are only a few families who can be regarded as domiciled at the post, and who do not go far away; the others go to a great distance. This is a very good thing, for the environs of Chekoutimi are so Drained of animals that they would Risk dying of hunger. If these lands were abandoned for some time, the Beaver would multiply, and animals would become more abundant; but that would be asking The Impossible from the savages. They would travel ten leagues to kill a beaver a year old, summer or winter, if they could find it. It is not, then, from these settled savages that much profit is expected; however They are not entirely useless. They make canoes for the inland trade; and we have them always at hand for the voyages that we are obliged to make. Among these savages there are some who would willingly go to Tadoussac, and it is of them that I have spoken in referring to the last post, saying they would be better off, and that they would furnish more profit.

2nd.  The People of Lake St. John are the sad remnants of an astonishing multitude of savages who inhabited the lands 60 or 70 years Ago. There only remain one large family, who work fairly well for the Interests of the post. They bring their Peltries at the time the ships arrive; and, after having tasted the brandy, they return to the lake, to live there during the summer upon Fish.

3rd.  Chomoukchwan was formerly dependent upon Lake St. John. The savages took their Peltries thither, or some one went after them, as is being done today. For some years the winter was passed there; but it has been seen to be a quite useless expense, and that it is sufficient to go there at the melting of the ice. This post is situated back of three Rivers. It would be a question of preventing the savages from going there; and, instead of 8 or 900 Martens that are generally obtained at that place, there would be many more. They are attracted thither by The brandy that they get in trade, and that is given them to take into the interior. That is a road which we have not hitherto been able to close.

The Agent of Chekoutimi sends thither a trader, whom he furnishes with merchandise, also two frenchmen and some savages of his post. At the end of july, all these men have returned. The savages are worthless, and one cannot place too little confidence in them; the journeys to three rivers have completely spoiled Them; and it would be a desirable achievement and a great profit for the post of Chekoutimi if they could be retained at home, and if the people of three Rivers could be prevented from sending the savages or frenchmen into the woods with liquor to trade with them. Desgroseilliers pursued this plan during the space of many years – and successfully, whatever Monsieur Cugnet[36] may say of it. The question now is, to find a man who can make the voyage every year in the capacity of a trader, either wintering at Chekoutimi, or repairing thither early in the spring; and I think that he will always be there in time, if he will leave Quebec at the end of April.

4th. The Mistassins are the best people in the world. They winter about 200 leagues from chekoutimi, toward hudson's bay, where some of them go to trade. Some bring their Peltries to the Post themselves, and a trader is sent to their country to receive those of the others and supply their needs. During the last three years, it is an Engagé of Tadoussac who makes the voyage; it is as fatiguing as that to Choumoukchwan, but it does not take so much time. As to that of choumoukchwan, there are nothing but rapids to ascend; on the other side, There are portages. It is from the Mistassins that the handsome marten-skins come – not so fine, indeed, as those of the River Moisy, but in greater numbers. As the agent of chekoutimi keeps an exact Account of what he Receives from every post, and gives a receipt for it to the traders, receiving one from them for the merchandise that he delivers to them, it will be easy to see what each separate district furnishes, and the profit that it returns.

5th. There remains one Place to which the agent began to Send goods last year, and whither I think they ought to be Sent this year also. It is Ounichtagan. If this enterprise can be made to succeed, it will be a great advantage; many savages from the interior will be attracted to that place. The Mistassins themselves will repair thither willingly, according to what I have heard; and thus the Frenchmen will afterward be relieved from making the voyage to the Mistassins, because Ounichtagan will be, so to speak, a Common rendezvous, to which all the savages of these regions will flock. The Agent of the islets may, perhaps, inveigh against this Establishment, saying that his savages will be taken away. What does it matter? We shall be sure to obtain their Peltries, and will not be exposed to deception; for there are some who take their Peltries to the islets, where they go to trade, and come straightway to chekoutimi to get goods on credit, – which is plain knavery on their part. This could be obviated by Establishing a post, and perhaps, afterward, by maintaining it in winter, At Ounichtagan.

It is also found that the consumption of food is great at Chekoutimi. The savages whose lands are in the Environs of the post come to the Warehouse when They fast in the woods, for I have already said that animals are rare there. 2nd, The many savages who Assemble for Trade in May, June, and july consume an extraordinary amount. I have with my own eyes seen them eat as much as ten quarts a day, and yet they were very moderately portioned. As the merchandise fails in the spring, on account of the goods that have to be Forwarded to the Mistassins and for chomoukchwan. It has happened often that these savages remain ten or twelve days at the Post to await the ship, and with it the merchandise of which they have need. Meanwhile, they have to be fed, and it happens then that everyone suffers. Both frenchmen and savages fast on account of the Delay of the ship, which ought to be at chekoutimi in the first days of June, at the latest; then the consumption would be less, because in two or three days everyone would be sent away. 3rd. When all these savages return to the interior, they are furnished with food, which is placed upon their account; and, if each family were only given the half of a quart, this would go far, but They carry away more. Thus it is very plain, by what I have just said, that this consumption of food is inevitable. 4th, in order to diminish it, It is necessary to have the ship depart early in the spring, in order that the savages may remain less time at the post. A feast is generally made for them at the arrival of the ship, and, rather than go without this feast, they would remain at the Post until the end of july; but when it is given, and it is given as soon as possible, each is seen to take his share, and plunge into the woods until the following spring.

I do not speak Here of the Construction of the sawmill in The River Pepawetiche, at half a League this side of chekoutimi; I will merely say that only two saws and two mountings are necessary to keep the mill in constant operation. Those whom I have Questioned upon this point, and who are well informed, have assured me that two saws kept going day and night will produce 140 or 150 planks every 24 hours. They also said that no advantage is to be derived from increasing the number of saws, and that they were returning to the other, – one mounting for each saw, and a saw in reserve. If the sawyers relieved each other by the quarter, The mill would continue going from the

15th or 20th of april until the 15th of November, – that is to say, more than six months. The planks could be carried in a raft to the Creek three leagues below the mill; all the ships can go there without danger, and The warehouse would be at Tadoussac. . . .

I pray Monsieur the Intendant to keep this memorandum to himself; and, if he judge it proper to make some extracts from it, not to say from whom It comes to him.

*april 5th, 1750.*

# VII

✳✳✳✳✳✳✳✳✳✳✳✳✳✳

## LETTER OF FATHER AUGUSTIN L. DE GLAPION
## TO MR. HUGH FINLAY, OF THE
## LEGISLATIVE COUNCIL
## (1788)

✳✳✳✳

MONSIEUR THE PRESIDENT:

I beg you to excuse me for having so long delayed my answer to the letter which you were pleased to write to me on the 26th of August last.

If you consider it indispensable that we should appear before The honorable Committee, we shall do so on the 15th of the present month, at The hour prescribed. But we shall not be able to say there what I have The honor to write you hereunder:

1st.   Since we have been under the English Domination, we have been, we are still, and we will always be submissive and faithful subjects of his Britannic Majesty. We venture to flatter ourselves that the English Governors who have commanded in this province would not refuse us Their Certificates of our fidelity and obedience.

2nd.   It seems, therefore, that in this instance it is not so much our persons as our temporal properties that are in question. Our properties or real estate have come to us from three different sources: 1st. The Kings of france have given us a portion of them. 2nd. Some individuals have given us another portion. These gifts were made with the view of providing for the subsistence of the jesuit Missionaries employed in instructing the savages and Canadians. The majority of the Fathers ceased to devote themselves to these charitable works only when they ceased to live; and those who survive them are engaged in the same work, and intend to continue the same until their deaths – which in The course of nature, cannot be very far distant. 3rd. Finally, our predecessors have, with Their own Money, purchased The third part of our property.

3rd. All our Title deeds, which are properly and duly recorded in the Record-office of The province, show that all these properties or real estate have always belonged to us in full ownership, and we have always managed and administered Them as our own, without opposition or hindrance.

4th. Our property was fully recognized in The Capitulation of Canada, signed in the camp before Montreal on the 8th of september, 1760, – inasmuch as, by article 35, Lord Amhurst permitted us to sell our real estate and effects, in whole or in part, and to send The proceeds to france.

In any case, Monsieur, we are in his Majesty's hands, and he will decide according to his good pleasure. But subjects and children without reproach can look forward to nothing but a favorable *treatment* – [*crossed out in Ms.*] decision from so benevolent a Monarch and so kind a father as his Majesty George III.

I have the honor to be, with profound respect,

Monsieur,

Your very humble and very obedient Servant,

AUGUSTIN L. DE GLAPION,

Superior of the jesuits in Canada.

*Quebec, September 10, 1788.*

# NOTES

## Part 1: The Beginnings of the Jesuit Mission to New France

[1] Charles Lalemant (1587-1674), a member of a Parisian legal family, was the first superior of the Jesuits in New France. Although he much disliked responsibility and life in the colony, he returned in 1634 after the English occupation. He was in charge of Notre Dame de Recouvrances, the chapel built by his friend Champlain at Quebec, until 1639. Thereafter he served as procurator in France for the Canadian missions.

[2] Jean de Brébeuf (1593-1649), the son of a noble Norman family, was a man of great practical intelligence and physical strength. He had found teaching in the Jesuit seminary at Rouen an unbearable strain, but became the most intrepid of missionaries. Having spent his first winter in New France among the Montagnais Indians, he was now about to found the Jesuit mission in the Huron country, where he was later martyred (see pp. 67-71).

[3] Paul le Jeune (1591-1664), a former Huguenot, had been a teacher of theology and rhetoric in France, and head of the Jesuit residence at Dieppe. As the second Jesuit superior at Quebec (1632-39), he re-established the mission there after the English occupation and proved himself a very able organizer and exponent of missionary expansion. He retired in 1649, disheartened by the destruction of Huronia and especially by the death of his friend Brébeuf.

[4] The widow of Louis Hébert, the first colonist to bring his family to Quebec (in 1617) and the first to cultivate a farm.

[5] Emery de Caen and his uncle, Guillaume, were Huguenots of a Rouen merchant family, the organizers (1621) of a trading and colonizing company which had absorbed Champlain's Company of Rouen and St. Malo. When le Jeune wrote, Jesuit influence had already helped to exclude Huguenot settlers from New France. Duplessis-Bochart, a naval officer, was to take part in the founding of Three Rivers (1634) and, as its governor, to die in its defence (see p. 140).

[6] Antoine Daniel (1601-48) had left his teaching post at the college of Eu to come to New France in 1632. He was to return from Huronia only once, in 1636-38, with some Huron boys whom he taught at Quebec. His death is described on pp. 64-66.

[7] Jean de Lauzon (1584-1666), notorious for his maladministration as governor (1651-56). At this time he was president of the Company of New France.

[8] Jacques Buteux (1611-52) had just come from France, nearly dying on the voyage. He spent most of his life in New France ministering to the Whitefish Indians at Three Rivers and on the St. Maurice River. An Iroquois war party killed him on his second journey up the St. Maurice.

## Part 2: The Mission to the Hurons

[9] *Sagamité* was the usual form in which the Indians ate corn. The corn was pounded into meal and boiled. Meat, fish, oil or – especially if the corn was green – other vegetables might be boiled with it. Father Chaumonot wrote that it tasted like wallpaper paste.

[10] François-Joseph le Mercier (1604-90) had gone to Huronia soon after his arrival at Quebec in 1635. He remained in that mission until its destruction, and also went among the Onondagas in 1656; the rest of his service was on the St. Lawrence. He was twice (1653-58, 1665-70) superior of the Canadian missions. He left about 1673 to go as superior to the mission in Martinique, where he died.

## Part 3: The Martyrdom of Huronia and the Mission to the Iroquois

[11] Barthélémy Vimont (1594-1667) had succeeded le Jeune as superior at Quebec, but the latter continued in charge of preparing the *Relation* until this year. It was under Vimont (1639-45) that the missions began to report success (see pp. 53-6).

[12] Jérôme Lalemant (1593-1673), Charles' younger brother, wrote parts of fifteen *Relations;* they show him as a man of unusual candour and wry humour. An energetic and dutiful missionary, his gifts were for teaching and administration. While in charge of the Huron mission he wrote a Huron grammar and supervised the translation of a catechism. He was superior at Quebec (1645-50) and then, after serving among the Montagnais, went to France as rector of the college at La Flèche. He returned as superior (1659-65) at the request of Laval, then newly appointed vicar-apostolic at Quebec. He became Laval's chief assistant in organizing the diocese of Quebec, which was formally established in the year after his death.

This extract records Father Jogues' first capture by the Mohawks. After a year as a slave he escaped, being helped by the Dutch with whom the Mohawks traded. He went twice more to the Mohawk villages, where he was killed in 1646.

[13] Paul Ragueneau (1608-80) was to climax thirteen years' service in Huronia by leading a party of refugees down to Quebec in 1650. There he succeeded Jérôme Lalemant as superior (1650-53), but proved tactless; the governor exiled him to Three Rivers. He served mainly among the refugee Hurons until returning to France in 1666. There he acted as agent for the Canadian missions.

[14] *Donnés* were lay volunteers who undertook to serve in the missions. Most were craftsmen; but the merchant in charge of supplying the Huron mission was a *donné* and so was the surgeon René Goupil (see p. 60).

[15] Gabriel Lalemant (1610-49), a nephew of Charles and Jérôme, was the youngest of six children, all but one of whom entered the religious life. He had been prefect of the Jesuit college at Bourges before coming to Quebec in 1646. After two years as a priest in the French settlements he went to Huronia – his first and last mission to the Indians. Physically weak since childhood, he nevertheless survived the tortures described in this letter for nineteen hours.

[16] Regnaut, a shoemaker, was a *donné* in Huronia and returned to France when the mission there was abandoned. He wrote this account for the Jesuits of Caen in 1678, when he was sixty-five years old.

[17] Charles Garnier (1605-49) came of a wealthy and noble Paris family, of whose other sons at least three also entered religious orders. Never robust, he came to Huronia in 1636 over the objections of his family. Even in the rigorous conditions of the mission he regularly mortified his flesh, wearing a belt of spur-rowels next to his skin. Particularly

adept at the Huron language, he was perhaps the most successful of the Jesuits in winning converts.

18 Noël Chabanel (1613-49) had been with the Huron mission for six years. He hated the privations, humiliations, and lack of privacy of the life and, although an accomplished scholar, could not learn to speak the Huron language. Nevertheless, he had taken a vow to spend his life among the Indians.

19 Simon le Moine (1604-65) was to make five journeys to the Iroquois, of which the first is described here. He had already served for twelve years in Huronia, going there directly from the college at Rouen.

20 Pierre Joseph Marie Chaumont (1611-95), while a Jesuit novice in Rome, was attracted to the Canadian missions by reading one of Brébeuf's narratives in the *Relations*. Besides the mission to the Onon-dagas, the beginning of which is described here, he ministered to the Hurons for half a century.

Claude Dablon (1619-97) was undertaking his first mission. His career was to exemplify the Jesuits' determination to extend their missions. When the Iroquois missions had to be abandoned because of renewed warfare (1658) he served on Lake St John and Lake Superior. Recalled (1670) to be rector of the College of Quebec and superior of the Canadian missions, he was responsible for sending Father Marquette to the Mississippi (see pp. 100-6) and edited the explorer's papers.

21 Claude Chauchetière (1645-1709) spent most of his life in New France (from 1679) at this mission. He wrote the life and painted the portrait of the most zealous of Iroquois converts, Catherine Tegakwita, to whom this letter refers.

## Part 4: The Western Missions and the Expansion of New France

22 Fort Nelson was not established by the Hudson's Bay Company until 1682, but the name dates from 1612-13 when the English explorer Sir Thomas Button wintered there.

23 Claude Jean Allouez (1622-89), except for Marquette the most far-ranging of Jesuit explorers, was on his first western venture. Vicar-general of the western missions, he served in them for a quarter of a century. Father Dablon credited him with baptizing over 10,000 Indians.

24 Alexandre de Prouville, Marquis de Tracy (1603-70), had just defeated the Iroquois, burning the Mohawk villages and ensuring the safety of New France for nearly twenty years.

25 René Ménard (1605-61), the pioneer of Jesuit western exploration, had served in Huronia and among the Iroquois before exploring (1660-61) the upper Great Lakes. Near the place referred to, Allouez founded the mission of La Pointe du St Esprit, the most westerly of Jesuit missions. It had to be abandoned in 1670 because of Sioux hostility.

26 Jacques Marquette (1637-75) had come to New France in 1666 and was sent at once to work with Allouez in the western missions. His eagerness for the journey here described arose partly from having been told by a band of Illinois in 1669 of a great river so long that they had never heard of its mouth. Marquette thought that it must lead either to Virginia or, more likely, to California.

27 These "kingdoms" of Tiguex and Quivira, with their supposed wealth, reflect the hopes of Spanish explorers. Coronado's search for them had taken place thirty years before Dablon wrote.

[28] Pierre le Moyne, sieur d'Iberville (1661-1706), born in New France and trained in the French navy, was a conspicuously successful commander in attacks on the English in Hudson Bay and Newfoundland. He was also a founder of the colony of Louisiana. In the year of this letter, ill health sent him back to France. He never returned to New France, dying on an expedition in the West Indies.

[29] Étienne de Carheil (1633-1726) had come to Michilimackinac in 1686, after twenty years as a missionary chiefly to the Iroquois. Shortly after this letter was written, the Hurons to whom de Carheil ministered were drawn away to a new French post at Detroit. De Carheil returned to Quebec, first burning the mission house (St Ignace) to prevent its desecration by pagan Indians. De Callières, to whom this letter was written, was the governor who in the preceding year had forbidden the use of brandy in the fur trade.

[30] In 1681 the governor of New France had been authorized to grant twenty-five licences to engage in the fur trade. The system did not prevent illicit trading; it was revoked in 1696 and the fur trade restricted to certain posts. Monopolies of the trade at the posts were leased, while the export of furs from Quebec was controlled by the Company of Canada, founded in 1701. It failed in 1706. Notwithstanding de Carheil's advice, the licences were revived in 1716 and never wholly abandoned.

## Part 5: The Jesuits at Quebec

[31] Marie Madelaine de la Peltrie (1603-71), left a widow at twenty-two, devoted herself and her considerable fortune to establishing the Ursulines in New France. She brought three nuns to Quebec, leaving them to join in the founding of Montreal (1642). Dissuaded by the Jesuits from going to Huronia, she entered her own convent at Quebec.

[32] The men here complained of, the most powerful of the colonists near Quebec, were members of the *Compagnie des Habitants* (1645-60), which had received a monopoly of the fur trade and was charged with governing and settling the colony. Robert Giffard, sieur du Beauport, had been the first landholder to bring out settlers in 1634. He was followed by Noël Juchereau, sieur des Chastellets; Noël's younger brother, Jean Juchereau, sieur du Maure, and his sons; and Guillaume Couillard, sieur de l'Épinay. Pierre Legardeur de Repentigny, one of several associates granted the seigneury of Beaupré, had been the wealthiest immigrant to Quebec in 1636; Father le Jeune had then regarded him as a model colonizer.

[33] Corneille's *Le Cid*? It had first been presented in Paris about ten years before.

[34] At a very rough reckoning, the livre may be taken as having had the purchasing power of a modern dollar.

[35] Claude Godefroi Coquart (1701-65) had come to New France in 1738. He had been in charge of the Saguenay mission for four years when he wrote the memoir from which this extract is taken. He is chiefly remembered for it and for another memoir commenting on La Vérendrye's famous western journey of 1741, which he shared as far as Michilimackinac.

[36] François Étienne Cuget was the farmer or lessee of the posts in the king's domain (i.e., outside the seigneurial grants). Father Coquart's memoir may have been requested as a check on his accounts by François Bigot, recently appointed Intendant.

# SUGGESTIONS FOR FURTHER READING

F. PARKMAN, *The Jesuits in North America* (Boston, 1897), remains the most serviceable narrative of the early Jesuit missions; it should be read along with a more recent and analytical work, J. H. KENNEDY, *Jesuit and Savage in New France* (New Haven, 1950). Among more specialized studies are J. DELANGLEZ, *Frontenac and the Jesuits* (Chicago, 1939); and W. AND E. MCL. JURY, *Sainte-Marie among the Hurons* (Toronto, 1954). The biographies of Jesuit missionaries are numerous: perhaps the best of them are *Saint among the Savages – the Life of Isaac Jogues* (New York, 1935) and *Saint among the Hurons – the Life of Jean de Brébeuf* (New York, 1949), both by F. X. TALBOT. T. J. CAMPBELL, *Pioneer Priests of North America, 1642-1710*, 3 vols. (New York, 1911), is a collection of short biographical sketches. G. T. HUNT, *The Wars of the Iroquois* (Madison, 1960) is indispensable. J. B. BREBNER, *The Explorers of North America, 1492-1806* (New York, 1933), will provide useful background. For general information on New France, readers may consult G. LANCTOT, *History of Canada*, Vol. I: *From Its Origins to the Royal Regime* (Toronto, 1963); or M. H. LONG, *History of the Canadian People*, Vol. I: *New France* (Toronto, 1942); or G. M. WRONG, *The Rise and Fall of New France*, 2 vols. (New York, 1928).

# THE CARLETON LIBRARY